Weehawken Public Library

49 Hauxhurst Avenue

Weehawken, NJ 07086

201-863-7823

Website: library.weehawken-nj.us

DEMCO

Military

Other books in the Careers for the Twenty-First Century series:

Aeronautics
Art
Biotechnology
Computer Technology
Education
Emergency Response
Engineering
Finance
Law
Law Enforcement
Medicine
Music
News Media
Publishing
Television

Careers
for the
Twenty-First
Century

Military

by Sheri Bell-Rehwoldt

LUCENT BOOKS

An imprint of Thomson Gale, a part of The Thomson Corporation

Detroit • New York • San Francisco • San Diego • New Haven, Conn.
Waterville, Maine • London • Munich

For my dad, Jerry Don Bell,
a retired army veterinarian

LIBRARY OF CONGRESS CATALOGING-IN-PUBLICATION DATA

Bell-Rehwoldt, Sheri.
  Military / by Sheri Bell-Rehwoldt.
    p. cm. — (Careers for the twenty-first century)
  Includes bibliographical references and index.
  ISBN 1-59018-398-3 (hard cover : alk. paper)
  1. United States—Armed Forces—Vocational guidance—Juvenile literature. I. Title. II. Series.
  UB323.B45 2005
  355'.0023'73—dc22

                                                          2005000672

Printed in the United States of America

Contents

Foreword

Young people in the twenty-first century are faced with a dizzying array of possibilities for careers as they become adults. However, the advances in technology and a world economy in which events in one nation increasingly affect events in other nations have made the job market extremely competitive. Young people entering the job market today must possess a combination of technological knowledge and an understanding of the cultural and socioeconomic factors that affect the working world. Don Tapscott, internationally known author and consultant on the effects of technology in business, government, and society, supports this idea, saying, "Yes, this country needs more technology graduates, as they fuel the digital economy. But . . . we have an equally strong need for those with a broader [humanities] background who can work in tandem with technical specialists, helping create and manage the [workplace] environment." To succeed in this job market young people today must enter it with a certain amount of specialized knowledge, preparation, and practical experience. In addition, they must possess the drive to update their job skills continually to match rapidly occurring technological, economic, and social changes.

Young people entering the twenty-first-century job market must carefully research and plan the education and training they will need to work in their chosen careers. High school graduates can no longer go straight into a job where they can hope to advance to positions of higher pay, better working conditions, and increased responsibility without first entering a training program, trade school, or college. For example, aircraft mechanics must attend schools that offer Federal Aviation Administration–accredited programs. These programs offer a broad-based curriculum that requires students to demonstrate an understanding of the basic principles of flight, aircraft function, and electronics. Students must also master computer technology used for diagnosing problems and show that they can apply what they learn toward routine maintenance and any number of needed repairs. With further education, an aircraft mechanic can gain increasingly specialized licenses that place him or her in the job market for positions of higher pay and greater responsibility.

In addition to technology skills, young people must understand how to communicate and work effectively with colleagues or clients from diverse backgrounds. James Billington, librarian of Congress, asserts that "we do not have a global village, but rather a globe on which there are a whole lot of new villages . . . each trying to get its own place in the world, and anybody who's going to deal with this world is going to have to relate better to more of it." For example, flight attendants are increasingly being expected to know one or more foreign languages in order for them to better serve the needs of international passengers. Electrical engineers collaborating with a sister company in Russia on a project must be aware of cultural differences that could affect communication between the project members and, ultimately, the success of the project.

The Lucent Books Careers for the Twenty-First Century series discusses how these ideas come into play in such competitive career fields as aeronautics, biotechnology, computer technology, engineering, education, law enforcement, and medicine. Each title in the series discusses from five to seven different careers available in the respective field. The series provides a comprehensive view of what it is like to work in a particular job and what it takes to succeed in it. Each chapter encompasses a career's most recent trends in education and training, job responsibilities, the work environment and conditions, special challenges, earnings, and opportunities for advancement. Primary and secondary source quotes enliven the text. Sidebars expand on issues related to each career, including topics such as gender issues in the workplace, personal stories that demonstrate exceptional on-the-job experiences, and the latest technology and its potential for use in a particular career. Every volume includes an "Organizations to Contact" list as well as annotated bibliographies. Books in this series provide readers with pertinent information for deciding on a career and as a launching point for further research.

Introduction

Building a Career in the Military

America's ability to remain a democracy is due, in large part, to its military. The five branches of the military—the U.S. Air Force, Army, Marine Corps, Navy, and Coast Guard—have been set up by the government to ensure that the United States has the military power necessary to defend its people, assets, and ideologies. The military is often used to protect people and governments in other countries as well, because the president and members of Congress believe in the importance of encouraging the spread of democracy and in building strong relationships with other countries to guarantee free trade. For example, the United States entered World War II, not because the battle took place on American soil, but because Adolf Hitler, the chancellor of Germany, and his Nazi Party threatened to erode world peace in their quest to take over Europe.

In order for the military to function effectively, it needs many people in many different kinds of jobs. According to the Department of Defense, in September 2004 there were nearly 1.5 million U.S. servicemen and -women serving on active duty around the world. Yet because people retire or exit the military each year, the military recruits a combined 365,000 people annually in more than 4,100 different job paths. While some recruits will be assigned to combat positions, defending military bases or serving in infantry positions that have direct interaction with enemy troops, 80 percent of military jobs are in noncombat occupations. Many electronics repairers, for instance, keep military computer systems up and running, and many members serve in military intelligence work in offices around the country, tracking enemy movements.

According to the U.S. Department of Labor, nearly 90 percent of new recruits in 2003 were recent high school graduates. That is not surprising, given that about 85 percent of the military is made up of enlisted personnel (those who enter without a college degree). The military has been successful in luring high school graduates with the promise of solid career training and generous educational benefits. Presently, the military is offering full reimbursement for the costs of college classes taken by recruits during active duty, up to a maximum of $250 per semester hour and $4,500 per year, for bachelor's, master's, and doctoral programs.

Marine recruits participate in a boot camp drill. The U.S. military hires approximately 365,000 people annually to work more than 4,100 different jobs.

And when they exit the military, enlistees can access an additional $38,000 toward a degree, courtesy of a tuition reimbursement program called the Montgomery GI Bill. This option is open to most service members who serve at least three years.

Enlistment and Promotion

When they join the military, high school graduates sign a legal agreement called an enlistment contract. This contract spells out how many years each new recruit must serve before being allowed to get out. This is a time commitment that new recruits must take seriously, as any military members who quit their unit or place of duty might be found guilty of desertion and punished. In times of war, desertion can be punishable by death.

Just as every branch has its own enlistment criteria, each branch has its own system for determining who gets promoted each year. Although good performance is a must for any military member hoping to get promoted, officers face stiff competition in getting promoted past the rank of major (or in the navy, past lieutenant commander). Air force, army, and Marine Corps officers typically enter the military at the rank of second lieutenant. They then progress to first lieutenant, captain, and major—with the lucky ones advancing to lieutenant colonel and colonel. In the navy and coast guard, officers enter as ensigns before progressing to lieutenant junior grade, lieutenant, and lieutenant commander.

Pay and Bonuses

The military uses the same pay scale across the branches, although some career fields receive additional special pay and bonuses because of their inherent danger. For 2005, Congress gave all military members a base raise of 3.5 percent. Military pay is based on grade (rank) and years in service. So new enlistees, entering at the rank of E-1, make $1,142 per month, yet receive $1,235 in the same grade after two years if they have not been promoted. Officer candidates, who enter the military with a college degree, enjoy significantly higher pay than enlisted members upon completing their officer training. New officers, entering at the rank of O-1, make $2,343 a month, unless they already have four years of active duty service as an enlisted or warrant officer. In that case, the starting pay is $2,948 per month. In addition to their base pay, enlistees and officers receive free base housing or off-base housing allowances, free on-base medical care, free food in on-base mess halls or an off-base Basic Allowance for sustenance if they do not have access to military meals.

In general, U.S. military members do not think that their pay is as competitive as it should be. Yet according to VetJobs.com: "when you add up the pay, allowances, 30 days paid vacation, training, holidays, medical and dental benefits, and divide that by their education, you will find that most will have a tough time matching their military 'package' in the civilian marketplace."[1]

Ongoing Training

Long before they can take advantage of these perks, new recruits must successfully pass their first major hurdle: an initial training period referred to as "boot camp." Here new recruits learn just how strong they are mentally and physically and if the military lifestyle is a good fit. Basic training varies in length between six and thirteen weeks. The army's basic combat training is nine weeks, the navy's boot camp is eight weeks, and the air force's basic military training is six short weeks of challenging instruction. The most difficult training program, however, is considered to be Marine Corps recruit training, which includes thirteen weeks of grueling tests that transform recruits into fully capable marines.

However, all the boot camps are demanding, as new recruits must absorb and become part of the military culture. They must memorize basic military facts and learn how to follow orders, march, and behave. Recruits are put through intense physical training and get yelled at a lot until they prove that they no longer think of themselves as individuals but as members of the most effective military in the world. Many recruits think of quitting boot camp; some do. Those who cannot buckle to authority are asked to leave. But those who remember that this difficult period is primarily a mind game, in which the military tries to tear down a recruit's civilian self to build it back up with a soldier's point of view, get through.

With this experience as their foundation, trainees then receive training specific to their military job. The American military provides some of the best training in the world. As many

U.S. troops engage in battle simulation exercises as part of their training, which continues throughout their military career.

enlistees get out of the military long before retiring, the military is an ideal place for high school graduates to gain solid job skills that they can take to the civilian sector. As well, the military instills recruits with a discipline and strong work ethic that many civilian workers never develop. As Don Laing, vice president of human resources at Litton PRC, a company that provides computer solutions for businesses, states: "Pride in doing the job . . . we experience that much more from people coming out of the military than from those who haven't had that experience."[2]

Job training continues throughout an enlistee's military career. Servicemen and -women routinely rotate to new job assignments, which require that they learn new skills. The military provides whatever training is needed, free of charge. Because the military must always remain combat-ready, it requires that service members keep up their physical fitness and spend a significant amount of time, even during peace, training for war scenarios and practicing drills. Pilots, for instance, are continually in the cockpit to ensure that their piloting skills stay sharp. Security forces members train for possible terrorist attacks. Even special forces members, the military's supersoldiers, train constantly so they have the confidence and skills to deploy, at a moment's notice, to a variety of situations and environments, from desert heat to arctic mountaintops.

A Lasting Connection

High school students can expect the military to provide them with numerous challenges and rewards. Though the work hours are long and the stress levels often intense, members of the armed forces gain significant intellectual stimulation and a high sense of satisfaction in knowing they are helping their country remain strong and free. The military also offers students the opportunity to broaden their experiences, travel the globe, and build friendships that may last a lifetime. The military is also where many young people learn to think for themselves, stretching to meet the responsibilities the military entrusts to them, often at just eighteen years of age. Because of these factors, service members forge an emotional and mental connection with their country that never disappears.

Many men and women in military service see their role as protecting the average citizen from external military threats. For them, then, a military career is not just a job, but a way of serving others. It is their way of making a difference. Thus, a military career is an ideal choice for those who enjoy discipline, responsibility, camaraderie, leadership, and the opportunity to serve as their country needs them.

Chapter 1

Intelligence Specialists

Military intelligence is very important to the security of the United States. Without the capability of monitoring enemy troop movement around the globe, the military would lose its ability to defend U.S. citizens, assets, and allies. Thus, the military relies heavily on its intelligence specialists to identify threats to the country's security. In his 2003 State of the Union address, President George W. Bush expressed his commitment to giving military intelligence specialists the tools needed to do the job: "Our government must have the very best information possible, and we will use it to make sure the right people are in the right places to protect all our citizens."[3]

With the explosion of global terrorism since September 11, 2001, the role of military specialists has become even more critical. Lives depend on their analysis. Military intelligence specialists analyze numerous sources of classified information. They might, for example, track the placement of an enemy's planes and tanks by looking at images captured by satellites. They might patch into foreign military radio communications to learn where and when an enemy plans to strike next. Or they might slip into the field and conduct in-person interviews with foreign locals to get details about suspected enemy activities in their areas.

Gathering Intelligence

These activities represent the three general areas of military intelligence. Military intelligence specialists who study visual images of the enemy are conducting Imagery Intelligence (IMINT). Intelligence specialists who monitor an enemy's communications are engaged in Signals Intelligence (SIGINT). And those who conduct field research are participating in Human Intelligence (HUMINT).

Though it is extremely dangerous to collect information in person, because of the possibility of being captured or killed, HUMINT remains an important means of gathering data. Technology, such as spy satellites, has eliminated much of the need for direct engagement, yet there are times when intelligence specialists must risk their lives and enter a war zone to obtain or verify information.

In many ways, technology is driving how the military gathers intelligence. IMINT specialists often study live images captured by U.S. spy planes to determine any immediate threats to U.S. ground troops. SIGINT, which was first used in the Civil War, has also grown in importance. SIGINT specialists, many of whom are proficient in two or more languages, have become experts at deciphering coded information hidden in an enemy's communications. Writes Don Stauffer in an article for the *Futurist:* "Today, every modern nation has the capability to monitor, jam, or otherwise interfere with an adversary's radio communications. Most

Military intelligence specialists study satellite images like these to monitor an enemy's movements.

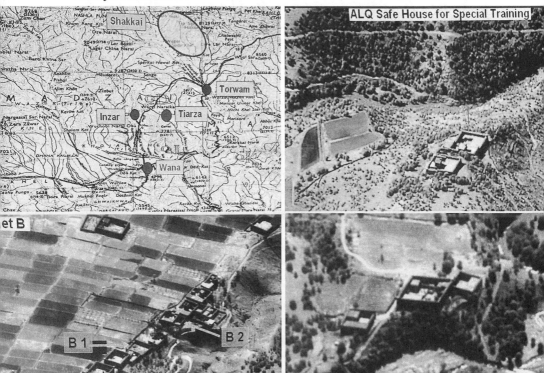

nations have also developed jam-resistant communications and intelligence-gathering equipment."[4] Thus, many SIGINT specialists focus on thwarting enemy access to U.S. military communications systems. To ensure their success, the military allocates billions of dollars from its defense budget for high-tech equipment and training.

Technology Guides Performance

In his book *The New Face of War*, author Bruce Berkowitz suggests that the continued effectiveness of the U.S. military depends not on the billions of dollars at its disposal, but on its ability to collect, communicate, process, and protect information using technological advances. He cites, as an example, the terrorist attack on the United States in September 2001:

> Information technology was the most important feature of the war between the United States and Al Qaeda. Communications networks held both armies together. Communications networks defined the battlefield. Al Qaeda won on September 11 because it had, to use military jargon, "information dominance." It knew where its targets were and maneuvered to attack them. We did not know where Al Qaeda was until it was too late.[5]

Thus, harnessing technology is critical to the United States' ability to stay in step with—or ahead of—its enemies. Better technology and equipment translate to better results. With these tools in hand, military intelligence specialists can then focus on the three other requirements of their job: identifying, analyzing, and communicating information. For example, the quicker that U.S. military intelligence specialists can collect and sift through information, the faster it gets to the field—and the better chance U.S. troops have of staying alive. Capt. George Melliza explains how cutting-edge technologies, such as minisatellites that travel with intelligence units when they deploy, help him to share information quickly:

> They have helped us to have uninterrupted intelligence collection capability during initial stages of conflict where

our troops haven't set up land line communications yet. I have also used the latest mapping software to map out our aircrew members' flying routes. I can then overlay our foes' locations and weapon capabilities onto these same maps. This has made it significantly easier for our pilots to visualize the danger in respect to where they are flying. The new software has made it much faster for me to do this compared to just six years ago where we were required to hand draw everything on maps with dry erase markers or pencils.[6]

Other high-tech tools include unmanned aerial vehicles (UAVs), the U-2S reconnaissance plane, and global positioning systems. Unmanned aerial vehicles are small spy planes that are piloted by a crew on the ground. Reconnaissance planes employ full crews who use the plane's onboard high-tech equipment to record and disseminate images of enemy targets while flying over them. Master Sgt. Mary Bechdel describes how these tools enable intelligence specialists to provide information to pilots thousands of miles away:

The U-2 flies over Iraq and the image is bounced through a secure communication link back to the States. An analyst looks at the image on a computer, writes a report, and sends a copy of the image/report through the secure communication link to the database or pilot back in Southwest Asia. They confirm the target with precision geo-coordinates and strike it with a smart bomb. This all happens within minutes.[7]

Learning the Job

With the military's growing reliance on technology, it is not surprising that Col. Jack Shanahan of the U.S. Air Force, an intelligence group commander, suggests that high school students are ideally suited to join this high-tech arena, due to their ease with electronics. He explains: "The pace of technological change today is incredible. . . . Adaptability is vital in today's military; many young people probably don't understand that they already have many of the skills needed to succeed in the military in this 'information age.'"[8] Students interested in a career in military

Predator Proves Its Worth

One reconnaissance tool now used by military intelligence specialists is the RQ-1 Predator, a medium-altitude, long-endurance unmanned aerial vehicle (UAV) system. Predators look like planes, but they are piloted from the ground. At 27 feet (8m) long and nearly 7 feet (2m) high, Predators have a wingspan of about 49 feet (15m). They are powered by a lightweight, four-cylinder snowmobile engine.

As Predators fly over a particular area, they transmit video and still-frame images from their nose-mounted cameras back to the intelligence specialist. Predators can pick up images in low light or at night via a variable aperture infrared camera, and in smoke, clouds, or haze via a synthetic aperture radar. Though they weigh more than 1,100 pounds (495kg), Predators can be easily disassembled, loaded into a container nicknamed "the coffin," and deployed around the world. Beyond being an effective spy tool, they protect the lives of the U.S. troops who would have to put their lives in danger to obtain similar information from the enemy. It was during Operation Iraqi Freedom that UAVs proved their effectiveness.

The RQ-1 Predator aerial vehicle is an unmanned spy plane that is piloted from the ground.

Military intelligence officers study maps and photographic images. Being able to read both of these types of documents is crucial for any intelligence career.

intelligence need a familiarity with computer software like Microsoft Word, PowerPoint, and Excel.

But comfort with technology is just the basis. High school graduates start their military intelligence careers by successfully completing basic military training—and proving they possess two important physical requirements: normal color vision and normal depth perception. They need both to work effectively with maps and photographic images.

Enlisted intelligence recruits then advance to specialized intelligence training to learn how the U.S. military gathers intelligence. Air force recruits complete their intelligence training at Goodfellow Air Force Base in Texas. Intelligence training for the Marine Corps and the navy occurs at the Navy Marine Corps Intelligence Training Center (NMITC) in Dam Neck, Virginia. The army conducts its intelligence training at Fort Huachuca, Arizona. Trainees learn about available intelligence resources, including satellites and computer intelligence systems. They are taught to analyze intelligence information, use maps and charts, and maintain intelligence databases and files. They also learn to catalog intelligence information properly so they can quickly retrieve older information to contrast it with new information.

Intelligence trainees are also taught to prepare and present intelligence graphics, reports, and briefings.

Every military branch differs in training and assignments. For example, in the navy, enlisted intelligence graduates move to their first assignment on large ships or with aircraft squadrons or intelligence facilities. If assigned to a ship, they help to defend against inbound threats by tracking enemy missiles. They also learn to operate and maintain the navy's global satellite telecommunications systems and to operate surveillance and altitude radar equipment such as the Identification Friend or Foe systems.

Officer's Route

Like enlisted specialists, officer candidates complete basic training. They only become officers upon successfully completing Officer Training School (OTS) if in the air force, or Officer Candidate School (OCS) if in the navy, the Marine Corps, or the army. Naval intelligence officers complete OCS in Pensacola, Florida, before attending NMITC or the Naval Cryptologic Officer Basic Course (NCOBC). At NCOBC, new intelligence

Navy intelligence graduates learn to operate global satellites like this one.

officers learn to analyze enemy communications messages to decipher their meaning.

In their first assignment, new naval intelligence officers might direct sea, ground, and aerial surveillance, analyze information, provide intelligence briefings, or help to minimize the enemy's ability to intercept and process the navy's electromagnetic signals. In the army, intelligence officers complete the Military Intelligence Officer Basic Course at Fort Huachuca. They specialize in one of six positions: imagery intelligence officer, all-source intelligence officer, all-source intelligence aviator, human intelligence officer, signals intelligence/electronic warfare officer, or counterintelligence officer. Officers who choose to specialize as counterintelligence officers, for example, learn to conduct investigations of individuals, organizations, installations, and activities to detect and assess threats to national security. The skills they practice include studying aerial photographs to identify troop movements and operating sensitive radios to intercept foreign military communications. They also become comfortable preparing maps, charts, and counterintelligence reports.

Building Expertise

Whatever their specialty, the most important skill that intelligence specialists develop is the ability to discern patterns and themes—to see the big picture—hidden in the avalanche of information they receive every day. One specialist in the field, for example, might report hearing rumors that a country is developing a new weapon. Using this tip as a guide, other intelligence specialists might spend many hours sifting through other sources to confirm that a weapon is being built, and its intended target. Military intelligence specialists learn to fit these bits of information together like pieces of a jigsaw puzzle.

An important skill they might develop is the ability to clearly "see" what the enemy has tried so carefully to hide from detection by satellites and other reconnaissance equipment. In her current role as an imagery analyst, Bechdel's job is to pick out threats, such as enemy weapons. Because of her training and on-the-job experience, Bechdel can look at aerial photographs of tree tops and see what is hidden below them. As though wearing special glasses, she can isolate the shapes of tanks and tents, which suggest that enemy troops are in the area. Bechdel describes how she is able to visually remove the clutter of the leaves:

> We're trained to look into the shadows for hidden aircraft, radar equipment, trucks, tents, antennas, people, etc. The shape of a shadow can tell you what type of electronic warning systems a site may have. Every type of equipment has distinguishing features that can be seen. It's like when someone puts a cover over their car to protect it. Even when looking from above, you can still narrow down what type of vehicle is under the cover by shape, length, width, and sometimes height. You can determine if it is an SUV, station wagon, or sedan. An analyst doesn't memorize all the different pieces of equipment; they compare what they see in the image to a line drawing or photo taken of the equipment. They compare whether there are wheels or tracks, the placement of the wings on the fuselage, or where the fins sit on the missile. They look pixel by pixel to figure out what they are looking at.[9]

After looking at the pictures, Bechdel writes a report and sends it along with the images to a database to be viewed by anyone interested in the information. As it takes new imagery trainees up to a year to be able to identify images, Bechdel says that it can be a challenge to communicate her analysis to those who have not had the benefit of her training. She compares this to showing a high school student several photographs of images that have been taken at very close range or at odd angles. With their untrained eyes, the students can only guess what the patterns represent.

Bechdel does not always work with static images. She also monitors live images, in real time. She explains how her review of live video from a UAV allows her to save the lives of U.S. troops:

> It's like watching a silent black and white movie. You know that U.S. forces will be in the area soon. You notice on one of the rooftops that a sniper is waiting; you can tell by the human shape and the reflection of the weapon from the sun. You text a message to the forces on the ground. You

Promotion in the Air Force

Upon joining the military, each enlistee signs a legal agreement called an enlistment contract. The contract signed by intelligence specialists typically commits them to serving eight years. Two to six of these years are spent on active duty, with the balance spent in the reserves.

Intelligence specialists typically enter the military at the rank of E-1. Each branch has its own system for determining who gets promoted. For instance, in the air force, enlistees can expect, on average, to be promoted after meeting these time-in-service (TIS) requirements: promotion to airman (E-2) in six months, to airman first class (E-3) in sixteen months, to senior airman (E-4) in three years, to staff sergeant (E-5) in under five years, to technical sergeant (E-6) in just under thirteen years, to master sergeant (E-7) in about seventeen years, to senior master sergeant (E-8) in just under twenty years, and to chief master sergeant (E-9) in about twenty-two years.

The air force uses the Weighted Airman Promotion System (WAPS) to determine promotion. This means that any enlisted military intelligence member at the level of E-5 is judged against all other same-ranked intelligence members. The air force promotes at the same percentage across all job functions. Thus, if the air force decides that the overall promotion rate to E-5 is 20 percent, only the top 20 percent of E-4s with the highest total WAPS points in each job will be selected for promotion. Promotions to E-8 and E-9 are made using a combination of WAPS points and a centralized promotion board. At the highest enlistment grades, performance reports matter most.

watch the scene unfold before you as your troops move in on the sniper and kill him. All this happens in real time and thousands of miles away on another continent.[10]

Capt. Brian Garino is another intelligence specialist who interacts directly with pilots, navigators, and aircrew members to provide them with the intelligence data they need to return safely from missions. He sums up his activities: "We tell them where

Intelligence specialists study satellite data on their computers. Being able to accurately identify enemy positions on satellite photos is a key skill for their jobs.

the bad guys are likely to be, what types of weapons they will likely use, and when would be the safer time to be at an airfield."[11] To provide this information, Garino relies on a classified internet called SIPRNET (Secret Internet Protocol Router Network), which includes Web sites from numerous intelligence organizations. Because the information on SIPRNET has been validated through several filters, Garino can accept it at face value. But if he receives "raw" data, which is information that has not been confirmed as factual, he must take the time to validate it before sharing it. This requires that he look for confirmation by studying other sources of information.

Dealing with Stress

Reviewing intelligence information quickly—and verifying that it is correct—ensures a stressful work environment. Intelligence specialists struggle daily to meet the expectations of superiors in a hurry for analysis. Sometimes this urgency is created because of a particular, event, such as 9/11. In general, however, intelligence specialists experience ongoing pressure to provide up-to-date analysis quickly because new information is continuously available. Thus, military intelligence specialists must be able to deal with ongoing stress—or face burnout. Airman Justin Calvaruzo of the U.S. Air Force describes what contributes to his stress level: "The demands placed on me are so much more mental than physical. Yes, the hours we work are long and tiresome, but the work itself is what makes our job so difficult. There is so much responsibility put onto our shoulders, and that burden is a heavy load to bear."[12]

Melliza notes that successful intelligence specialists share some common attributes, including patience and focus. They need both, as it can take a considerable amount of time to identify an enemy's patterns. The fact that the enemy is always changing tactics and getting smarter as it learns from U.S. actions does not make an intelligence specialist's job any easier.

How intelligence specialists get along with others at work also contributes to whether they feel satisfaction on the job. It is important that they not only do their jobs well, but do so with strong interpersonal skills, flexibility, and a positive attitude. Shanahan explains: "It's crucial to get along with people; not everyone is a people person, but your ability to keep going up [get promoted] is, as it would be outside the military, dictated to a large extent by an ability to communicate effectively and get along with peers, subordinates, and bosses."[13]

Preparing Early

Even in high school, students can hone the interpersonal skills and out-of-the-box thinking they will need for a career in military intelligence. Because intelligence specialists need a sharpened mind that can easily sift through information, Air Force Master Sgt. Michael Welch suggests that students take classes that require critical thinking, research, and analysis, such as politics, philosophy, science, and literature. He also suggests that students take computer technology classes to gain a basic understanding of programming and networks. Also helpful are classes in world history, foreign languages, and social studies and cultural issues, because they give students an awareness of events and ideologies that create tensions around the globe.

Proficiency in speaking to groups is also important, so students are encouraged to participate in public speaking and debate classes. These classes prepare students to give presentations to large numbers of people. Their ability to do so with confidence is important, notes Melliza, because they may address groups that include their squadron commander and high-ranking members of the Department of Defense.

Security Clearance Hurdle

Due to the sensitive nature of their jobs, military intelligence members must gain a top secret security clearance before being allowed to work in their first assignment. When a person receives a security clearance, it means that the military has determined that he or she is trustworthy and loyal to the United States and may be given access to critical information. A top secret clearance—the highest clearance possible—is required for any military member handling information that, if leaked, could cause exceptional damage to U.S. national security. Since the military reviews an applicant's previous ten-year history, any high school student considering this career field must keep out of trouble.

To gain the top secret security clearance, military intelligence specialists must pass an extensive background check called a Single Scope Background Investigation. Applicants are asked to identify where they have lived, worked, and gone to school. They are asked about their family members, their military history, and any police record. Though they may be just out of high school, applicants are asked to disclose any financial records they may have established, foreign countries they have visited, and contact information for three people who know them well. During in-depth interviews, these coworkers, employers, friends, and neighbors are asked their opinion of the applicant's trustworthiness, and whether the U.S. military should extend its trust. The applicant is also personally interviewed.

Pay and Advancement

A security clearance has other benefits, including higher pay, particularly when service members look for jobs in the civilian sector, which they often do since the military pays significantly lower salaries than most private companies. Although military promotions guarantee raises, newly enlisted security specialists make significantly less than new officers. In 2005, for example,

Security Clearance Mandatory

To work in military intelligence, enlistees need first to obtain a security clearance. Receiving a security clearance means that the military has determined that a person is trustworthy and loyal to the United States and may be given access to critical information. There are three types of military security clearances: confidential, secret, and top secret. Information is considered confidential if it could cause damage to national security if leaked, and it is considered secret if it would cause serious damage. A top secret classification is applied to information or material that could be expected to cause grave damage to national security if leaked without authorization.

Current laws state that anyone who has been convicted of a crime and sentenced to a prison term for more than a year will not receive a top secret clearance. Neither will applicants found to be addicted to a controlled substance, mentally incompetent (this judgment will be made by a mental health professional appointed by the Department of Defense), or discharged from previous military service under dishonorable conditions. Applicants must not lie to hide any of these disqualifiers; anyone found to falsify or knowingly conceal information faces up to five years in prison and a $10,000 fine.

Top secret clearances are typically granted within six to eight months. Yet the process can take significantly longer if an applicant has lived or worked overseas, has traveled frequently overseas, or has family living in other countries.

Those being discharged or retiring from the military with a top secret clearance leave with a marketable asset. They often find jobs quickly with federal agencies such as the Central Intelligence Agency, Federal Bureau of Investigation, and the National Security Agency. Private companies that do business with the government also like to hire ex-military personnel with top secret clearances, because obtaining new clearances for employees can cost the companies thousands of dollars.

the monthly pay is $1,142 for an enlisted E-1 and $1,456 for an E-3. A new army officer, as an O-1 (second lieutenant), receives $2,343 monthly, but that pay jumps to $3,124 as an O-3 (captain). This gap continues to widen over the years. However, an enlistee who obtains a college degree has the option of applying to become an officer.

Many officers, however, find they are unable to advance past the rank of major (O-4), due to competition for limited slots. Because salary is determined by rank and time in service, however, an O-4's monthly salary is based on a sliding scale, between $3,553 and $5,582, according to the 2005 military pay scale.

Some officers, like Melliza, develop formal plans early to ensure they have the best shot at being promoted. Melliza is careful to maintain a positive attitude so that his superiors perceive him as committed and worthy of promotion. To back that perception, he showcases his leadership skills by volunteering for special assignments. He has also continued his education, to ensure that other candidates do not gain a competitive edge over him in that area. He plans to obtain his master's degree and gain entry into the Air Command Staff College in-residence program, a year-long program that prepares majors for additional leadership responsibility and command.

Garino agrees that upon reaching the rank of major, there is significant pressure to distinguish oneself from others at the same rank, but adds that enlisted specialists must also prove their worth: "Because the military is such a large organization you have to make a name for yourself and set the example in everything you do. If not, you are just a number and you can be overlooked for opportunities. Motivation and initiative are key to a successful career in intelligence. Someone who shows the initiative around our workspace will get noticed and be given more opportunities."[14]

Outlook and Opportunities

There are more than twenty-five thousand intelligence specialists and ten thousand intelligence officers in today's military, and the field is expected to grow. A stint in military intelligence, whether for a few years or longer, gives high school students solid skills that they can transfer to many civilian intelligence opportunities—in no small part because of their top secret security clearance. Security clearances are very difficult to acquire outside of the military; thus they are extremely valuable. But there are other benefits to a job in military intelligence. For example, the military currently allows high school graduates to obtain a college education, at little or no cost to them, while they are in service. They also receive ample training, which develops their marketable job skills.

Some intelligence specialists cite stress, the difficulty of advancement, and the comparatively low pay as reasons for leaving the military to take higher-paying civilian jobs. Fortunately, their well-honed analytical skills give them the opportunity to transfer to research or business planning, with job titles such as marketing manager or advertising executive. Or, if they have expertise in studying human nature, they might consider becoming lawyers, social workers, psychologists, counselors, or media reporters.

Yet many intelligence specialists do choose to stay with the military until retirement because they enjoy the leadership opportunities they are given—and find personal satisfaction in helping America to stay free. They also cite the diversity of assignments, travel, and training as positive aspects of their careers.

Chapter 2

Security Forces

Military security forces, composed of enlisted personnel and officers, play a critical role in the military. They are trained to take control of any situation that threatens physical harm to the military's equipment, resources, and people. They have the same authority on their military bases that civilian police officers have in their respective jurisdictions. With their training in base defense, security, and law enforcement, military security specialists perform many tasks. Some stop unauthorized personnel from driving onto military bases and gaining access to buildings that house classified information or planes worth billions of dollars. Others direct vehicle and pedestrian traffic or investigate accidents and crimes. Still others help with disaster and relief operations.

There are also many opportunities to specialize. Experienced security specialists with proven leadership skills might volunteer for special roles such as partnering with dogs trained for the military's canine programs, guarding U.S. embassies in foreign countries, or protecting the president and other officials as they travel. Another dangerous job security specialists might volunteer and train for is aerial transport protection. As flight crews fly in and out of unsecured foreign locations, the security forces guard aircraft and crew from sniper attacks.

To be successful in any of these roles, military security forces members must approach their tasks with a commitment to high job performance. Air Force Security Officer Christopher Castaneda emphasizes that his actions inspire respect among other military members: "We emplace extremely strict standards on ourselves to make sure that we conduct ourselves above reproach and we continually train to make sure that we are better than just proficient. We MUST be the best: the best trained, the best equipped, and the best led—this is what allows us to gain that trust and respect."[15]

Learning the Basics

Every security specialist learns how to defend and protect U.S. assets, such as expensive high-tech equipment. They train in order to respond efficiently to whatever security issues come up during their shifts. For example, they might hand out parking citations, man the entry and exit points of their assigned military base, respond to calls of domestic disputes, or conduct surprise drug raids in the on-base dormitories. New military security specialists are given levels of authority that their peers working in civilian jobs do not experience until they are promoted into management roles. It is the military's commitment to training that makes this possible.

An army security guard protects the Jordanian embassy in Iraq. He is one of many soldiers trained for such duties.

An air force security guard stands watch over a Stealth bomber. Though they receive all kinds of training, today's security specialists concentrate on ways to respond to terrorism.

Military security training builds on the discipline and military knowledge that security specialists and officers acquired in basic training. Those in army and Marine Corps security forces complete the Law Enforcement Military Police Course at the United States Army Military Police School in Fort Leonard Wood, Missouri, while air force security forces train at the Security Forces Academy at Lackland Air Force Base in San Antonio, Texas. There, they learn deadly force techniques and various guard duties. They also learn how to secure a crime scene, how to conduct surveillance, and how to search individuals, buildings, and vehicles.

Unfortunately, with the rise of terrorism around the globe, U.S. security forces specialists now spend many hours training in how to respond to terrorist attacks. They learn, for example, how to handle chemical, biological (e.g., anthrax), and nuclear threats. Lt. Col. Glyn Bolasky notes that in high-stress situations, military police are able to revert to their training automatically: "That's why it's so important to train serious and hard. The brain works fast in a life or death situation, and you'll recall things you were taught. Your training will give you the ability to assess situations quickly and make better decisions."[16]

Military security forces officers complete three additional months of training at Security Forces Officer Technical School. In addition to drilling in security issues, they hone their leadership skills to gain the credibility to lead their troops. Graduates are expected to be competent leaders on their first day on the job. Castaneda explains: "As a Security Forces Officer, I was leading a flight [group] of 40 from day one. There is no other job in the Air Force where you get that kind of leadership responsibility right off the bat."[17]

Teaming with Canines

With several years of solid security experience behind them, specialists can apply for jobs to build special areas of expertise. In doing so, they increase their value to the military. Those who enjoy working with dogs, for example, might volunteer to be canine handlers. This is a challenging assignment as it can be difficult to work with a dog.

The U.S. military has been using working dogs since World War II. Today, it is the air force that trains the dogs and handlers, and army veterinarians who keep the dogs fit. About twenty-three hundred dogs have been distributed to the military branches to conduct searches of vehicles, open spaces, and buildings and to perform tracking searches for lost or wanted persons. Military canine handlers and their dogs also partner with the Secret Service to offer protection for the president and visiting dignitaries.

Most military canine handlers in the air force are enlisted E-5s (staff sergeant) or E-6s (technical sergeant). As handlers eventually get promoted beyond these ranks and move out of the program, the dogs are paired with new handlers every few years. Each dog must learn to work with and trust the new handler. But for the period they are together, the handler and dog become a tight unit. Canine handlers gain immense satisfaction from helping their dogs grow in skill and success.

Since September 11, 2001, about five hundred dogs have been trained each year at the Defense Department's Military Working Dog Program at Lackland Air Force Base. Security members new to the canine program learn to work with their dogs and practice giving commands. The task can be challenging, particularly if the dog's performance is uneven or the dog has a strong personality. Staff Sgt. Michael Smith, a kennel master at McChord Air Force Base in Washington, explains: "New handlers need to have patience, because a dog can have a good day in training one day and a horrible day in training the next. They

Sea Creatures Defend Against Underwater Intruders

Not all the military's security specialists are human; some, in fact, are mammals. The U.S. Navy uses the bottlenose dolphin and California sea lion to protect ports and ships around the world. Due to their intelligence, underwater abilities, and keen sense of hearing, these mammals are ideal for patrolling underwater, searching for intruders. Dolphins possess a sophisticated sonar system, and sea lions can see in low-light environments and maneuver themselves in tight spaces. Both can conduct numerous dives without getting decompression sickness like humans do. The mammals detect underwater mines that could damage or sink U.S. military ships. After mines are detected, human divers, trained in security tactics, disarm the mines. The navy does not train the mammals to carry weapons or destroy ships. Navy sailors and civilian employees train and care for the animals. When the security team deploys to various assignments, an army veterinarian travels along to care for them. Daily, the veterinarian inspects the animals for nicks and cuts.

Dolphins are one sea animal the U.S. Navy uses to protect the world's ports and ships.

Soldiers and a specially trained dog patrol the streets of Baghdad in Iraq.

also can't be afraid of the animal. We have a term called 'run down leash.' It means that if you're afraid, your fear will run down the leash and the dog will know."[18] Like Smith, all canine handlers learn that the dogs work best when they view their work as a game. Thus, one of the key duties new handlers learn is how to motivate their dogs. This typically means offering the dogs more play time for working hard. It also means adjusting a dog's environment or schedule to accommodate the dog on days when it is unable to focus.

When canine handlers deploy to overseas assignments, their dogs go with them. Several hundred military dogs currently work in Iraq and Afghanistan as patrol dogs. Since dogs have a sense of smell up to ten times stronger than a human's, one of their most important duties is detecting explosives. Dogs also instill fear in people, which doubles their effectiveness as a strong psychological deterrent. Smith believes that the highly trained canines have a distinct advantage over other military weapons: "The best thing about the dogs is that they are a weapon you can call back once you shoot it."[19]

Snipers and Countersnipers

Another limited specialty area that military security forces might volunteer for is the role of sniper or countersniper. This is a key military position in times of war. Snipers use rifles to protect U.S. forces and equipment from surprise enemy attack. This role takes exceptional skill, as snipers must be able to spot and shoot enemy soldiers from great distances. Though they are expert marksmen, the sniper's main job is reconnaissance. Snipers look for key targets, such as pilots, armor drivers, and communications operators, and kill them with a single shot. Such a sniper attack often causes the enemy forces to panic. Conversely, countersnipers are security specialists who scout for enemy snipers. Their job is to take out the snipers before they have an opportunity to cause harm to U.S. forces and equipment. Air force countersnipers have an important job: They guard multimillion dollar military aircraft from enemy snipers in places like Iraq, Bosnia, and North Korea. Their job is to prevent a sniper's bullet, launched from a mile away, from punching through the side of a U.S. plane, blowing up its wing fuel tank, or destroying its flight equipment.

According to an article in *Airman* magazine, this kind of attack destroyed nearly four hundred U.S. and allied aircraft in Vietnam and damaged more than a thousand others. Marine Gunnery Sgt. Carlos Hathcock II, who was recognized as the military's best-known sniper because of a kill he once made in Vietnam from a distance greater than twenty-two football fields, once said: "The most deadly thing on the battlefield is one well-aimed shot."[20]

Like many others, security forces specialist Larry Knoll has been deployed to Iraq. But because of his exceptional skills in countersniping, his commander was able to use him at the airfield to beef up security—and send him out on patrol to hunt for snipers toting shoulder-fired surface-to-air missiles capable of targeting a cargo plane from six miles away. Knoll describes the satisfaction he felt in preventing any interruption in the service of the runway: "We patrol well past the front lines, so we can take out a target well before it can threaten our aircraft or people. We have to keep a sharp eye open all the time."[21] Though this is a dangerous job, for some it offers the ultimate challenge.

Snipers work in teams, waiting hours or days for the perfect target. The "shooter" pulls the trigger after the "spotter" has helped plan the shot. Spotters carry a special scope that is more powerful than the scope on the sniper's rifle. The spotter's most important job is to protect the shooter, so the spotter also carries an automatic assault rifle. Some sniper teams are expertly camouflaged by ghillie suits, which make them appear as half-human, half-shrub. Though the canvas uniforms are painted to match their environment, the teams often stick twigs and leaves in the netting of their suits to camouflage them further. Snipers also make ghillie suits for their rifles. One army Ranger sniper notes: "With a good ghillie suit you could hide in a yard and people wouldn't be able to see you."[22]

Most security members graduate from the five-week U.S. Army Sniper School at Fort Benning, Georgia, or one of the Marine Corps's sniper schools. Trainees receive a long-range rifle and other equipment. They learn the principles of ballistics, and how wind and gravity affect a bullet. And they learn to move

A sniper peers through the scope of his rifle while his spotter searches for a target. Snipers often work in teams and sometimes wait days for their targets.

slowly and methodically so they can silently stalk their target. They perfect the art of lying completely still for hours, despite rain, heat, or crawling insects. They know their lives and the success of their mission depend on their going undetected.

These security specialists also hone their observation skills. In a common class exercise, they sketch items, such as pieces of equipment at a target site, that they observe through binoculars. In these tests they must also be able to identify what is missing or added after their instructors change the setting. These memory exercises continue daily, with students being asked hours later about particular objects. One Ranger sniper says that the exercise rewired his brain: "Even just driving down the road now I see weird little things on the side of the road that a lot of people wouldn't really notice."[23]

To pass the class, security forces members must hit fourteen targets, at distances from 328 to 1,094 yards (300 to 1,000m), in day and night settings. Students must also complete the army physical fitness test, which involves running, push-ups, and sit-ups.

Ravens

A third specialty area open to security specialists is aerial transport protection. In this role security specialists protect flight crews and cargo on the ground, often in hostile territory. The air force refers to these highly trained individuals as "Ravens." Though it is their job to offer protection, Ravens always hope to prevent conflict. Thus, Ravens do not immediately brandish weapons. This mind-set often enables Ravens to prevent conflict, says Master Sgt. Benjamin Harper, an instructor at the Phoenix Raven course:

> We're not going to be doormats. We want Ravens to defend themselves, our resources and people, but we don't want them throwing down the gauntlet every time somebody walks up to them. Instead of saying "Halt" whenever a stranger approaches, we teach them to say, "Hi. How you doing?" . . . It's a change of mindset for some cops. Traditionally, we've been taught to be authoritative, to challenge and to take charge of a situation. Sometimes that only aggravates a situation.[24]

City in a Box

Security forces personnel routinely deploy to foreign locations. During these temporary foreign assignments, many of them miss the hot meals, hot showers, and comfortable beds they leave at home. These inconveniences, coupled with other mental and physical stresses of war, can significantly affect their morale. One tool the army has begun using to make security personnel more comfortable is the Force Sustainment System. These are tent cities that can take sixty people a full week to set up. These "cities in a box" can be tailored to various conditions to meet the housing needs of up to 550 troops. The city's basic building block is the Tent Extendable Modular Personnel, or TEMPER. Each system is equipped with a heating and air-conditioning unit. This feature is appreciated by troops operating in desert locations, where daytime temperatures can soar beyond 120°F (49°C). Though the tents work well during short deployments, the army is looking to create hard-wall systems for long-term deployments.

At the Phoenix Raven course, which is two weeks long and held at the Air Mobility Warfare Center at Fort Dix, New Jersey, security members learn hand-to-hand self-defense tactics and antihijacking procedures. They also learn how to survey airfields and how to use tools such as pepper spray, a 200,000-volt stun gun, and batons, including a collapsible baton called an ASP. About 30 percent of the security specialists who attempt to become Ravens fail the course.

Since the Raven program's inception in 1997, Raven team members have accompanied more than four thousand missions, detecting, deterring, and countering threats to aircraft. Frequent travel is a given, as missions typically involve only short stints on the ground to drop off cargo or personnel. According to pilot Derek Orling, Ravens normally travel with large aircraft and remain on call to travel anywhere in the world in under twenty-four hours:

In the last year I've been in over 50 countries. We fly to Baghdad, Iraq, and Kabul, Afghanistan, numerous times

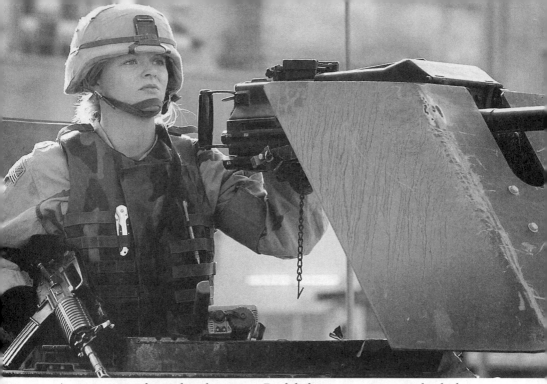

A security guard patrols a downtown Baghdad street in an armored vehicle, one of several duties such guards perform.

each month. I've been to Tokyo, Japan, Beijing, China, Vietnam, remote airstrips in Columbia, Panama, Nigeria, Australia, and numerous other countries in the last year. Also, I recently flew a mission which assisted in the removal of nuclear components for which I received a medal.[25]

During Raven missions, security members know there is always the chance they will be physically harmed. Orling says that he plays a mind game to dispel any anxiety he feels about his personal safety, as he is unwilling to stop doing a job he loves:

On a Raven mission, you can't tell yourself that you're the only one, along with your two team members, that are there to guard the aircraft. It's a little daunting to think that you're sitting in the middle of a remote landing strip and you're the last line of defense if somebody decides to make a statement for their cause by blowing up a U.S. aircraft. You just gotta do your job and if something happens, you deal with it.[26]

Generalists Find Challenge

Security forces do not have to volunteer for special roles to experience challenging and satisfying military careers. Their roles change with every assignment—especially when they deploy to overseas assignments. Their duties expand significantly during deployments, because the rules of conduct differ significantly from those they follow at their home bases. Technical Sgt. Brian Curtis explains that during deployment, air force security members and officers become "Defenders of the Force": "The flashes [pins] we wear on our berets have 'Defensor Fortis' on them. We patrol the base, handle prisoner control, offer protection for generals when they visit, and investigate things."[27]

Similarly, deployed army and Marine Corps military police conduct battlefield control, prisoner control, and preserve law and order. Often, they are called upon to guard important travel routes. While on deployment in Iraq in 2004, Sgt. Mark Estes daily helped to monitor a main supply route. This involved locating hidden explosives on the road, watching for thrown grenades, taking care of vehicle breakdowns, and monitoring local traffic: "The Iraqis know the routes we use and conceal IEDs (improvised explosive devices) along this and other supply routes almost every day. IEDs are one of the biggest problems. They are getting more sophisticated and more deadly. Sometimes you can't even tell if an IED is a piece of debris—or what it is."[28] Estes adds that the danger of clearing these explosives is compounded by local residents' frustration at the army's caution. Part of a deployed security specialist's or officer's job in Iraq, then, is trying to build a relationship of trust with the Iraqis, so they understand that U.S. military personnel are trying to protect them, not inconvenience them.

Job Performance Matters

Regardless of the tasks they handle, military security specialists must enjoy working in a job that demands that they be of service to many other people, and do it to the best of their ability—or face being disciplined. Specialists who are interested in continuing in the security field, but who are having trouble maintaining a positive attitude, are given ample opportunity to improve. Others are allowed to cross-train to other areas of military service, if there are job openings in those fields.

However, continued unsatisfactory job performance can lead to expulsion from the military. Castaneda contends that most on-the-job problems start because of personal issues, such as substance abuse or trouble managing personal finances. To ensure that enlistees and officers are successfully doing their jobs and meeting expected standards of conduct, the military carefully reviews and documents their overall performance at least yearly.

The U.S. Air Force, for example, uses the Enlisted Performance Report (EPR) and the Officer Performance Report (OPR). All EPRs and OPRs are placed in the security member's permanent military file, with the most recent carrying the most weight. If the current EPR or OPR evaluation is not good, it will affect the member's ability to get promoted. Poor evaluations can also lead to reduction in pay and disciplinary action. Castaneda gives an example:

We recently had a great troop [airman] go through a divorce, get drunk, and get a DUI [Driving Under the Influence of alcohol or drugs]. He was given an Article 15, which resulted in a reduction in rank, some lost pay, and he was not allowed to drive for a year. We also had to write a Referral EPR, which is an EPR that either has a bad comment, in this case about his DUI, or is marked down in one area. The referral EPR allows the member a chance to defend him or herself before a final rating is given. He's a stellar troop, so he'll be able to recover from it, but in the meantime he'll suffer the consequences.[29]

Military police conduct is so closely monitored because of the authority these men and women have. In addition to integrity, there are other attributes successful security specialists and officers need to display. These include sound reasoning and problem-solving skills and the ability to speak clearly, to work well as a team, and to approach situations creatively in order to gain control and a positive outcome. To beat burnout and remain effective, security forces members also need to remain empathetic and patient. Curtis explains:

You never know what you will see since we deal with people on a daily basis. There are many times when people scream and complain to us, but you have to keep your cool and always be bigger than them. It's professionalism. A good cop doesn't get mad at a kid mouthing off to him; he takes the time to consider if the kid is having a bad day.[30]

Security Clearance a Must

Because the military holds security forces members to a high ethical standard, it requires them to have security clearances. These clearances are dispensed when the security member is found to be sufficiently honest, trustworthy, reliable, emotionally stable, and financially responsible. Jobs in Air Force Security Forces, for example, require a Sensitive Job Code of "F." This means that in a list of background questions, security specialists and officers have been able to answer "no" to questions involving use of marijuana in the last six months, prior alcohol dependency, attempted

Deserters Receive Punishment

Since 9/11, frequent deployments have caused some security specialists and officers to dread the long separations from their lives back home. Though the separation from family and friends is hard and the living conditions at these temporary duty stations are often uncomfortable, these security members do not have the option of deciding they will not go. Refusing to accept these assignments is considered an act of desertion.

According to the Uniform Code of Military Justice, deserters are those in the military who leave their assignments without permission from their superiors and with the intent of not returning to their duties. Thus, if any recruit hates his or her job, dislikes the military lifestyle, or is afraid of harm or death because of where he or she is assigned, he or she cannot decide to arbitrarily quit his or her military commitment. Desertion is the worst thing a member of the military can do because any person found to be a deserter, or even attempting to desert, may be punished. In time of war, this punishment could be death. If the United States is not at war, the military court can decide any punishment for desertion, except death.

suicide, personal bankruptcy, and expulsion from school for misconduct in the last two years. The basic army requirement is a confidential security clearance, which is the lowest of three possible security clearances. In contrast, the Marine Corps requires a secret security clearance. Yet some of its security positions, including that of criminal investigator, require a top secret clearance, the highest clearance level possible.

Because these clearance reviews look at police records, high school students interested in a military security career need to stay out of trouble, says Orling: "That's not saying you have to be a monk living in your bedroom, but when you're out having fun, be smart about it. A simple night out to a party or out on the town can affect the rest of your life."[31]

Explore the Field Early

Even in high school, students can build skills and experience to prepare for a career in military security forces. Technical Sgt. William Smith believes that one of the best ways is by learning to multitask, since juggling multiple projects builds flexibility and leadership skills. Curtis stresses the importance of learning to tolerate other viewpoints, developing good study habits, and getting into good physical shape. He suggests that students take high school courses in government, behavioral science, computers, and communication.

To gain insight into police activities, students can also contact their local police department to participate in a Ride Along program. These programs allow the public to observe police officers in action from the safety of their police cruisers. Each Ride Along program has a minimum age requirement. The Menlo Park Police, in Menlo Park, California, for example, allows teens as young as fifteen to ride along with an officer for four hours. This police force requires a form signed by a parent, possibly a background check, and a promise that the rider will not step out of the cruiser or interact with suspects, victims, or witnesses without the officer's permission.

Salary

Based on the 2005 military budget, an enlisted security specialist, with three years' experience, reaches the rank of E-4 and earns a monthly base salary of $1,612. At five years, as an E-5, their base salary is $1,759. Officers who are O-4s are paid a base salary of $3,553 and as O-5s (lieutenant colonel) receive a base salary of $4,118. Though pay is one reason that enlistees cite for leaving the military for civilian jobs, those who stay until retirement appreciate the financial cushion they take with them, including continued medical benefits and a healthy percentage of their base salary. Technical Sgt. (E-6) William Smith explains: "Right now I plan on retiring at the young age of 43 with 24 years of active military service behind me. I will receive 54 percent of my final base pay every month for the rest of my life."[32]

Future Outlook

There are about 33,500 specialists and 3,500 officers working in military security, and this field is expected to grow. If they perform their duties well and can deal with the stress, enlisted security specialists and officers enjoy long, diverse careers. A benefit of their security training is that they develop marketable skills that they can transfer to civilian jobs. Many of those who choose to leave the military find jobs quickly as police officers, deputy sheriffs, state troopers, investigators, and air marshals. Others are snapped up by the Federal Bureau of Investigation, which fully appreciates their experience. The military training these men and women receive, coupled with their commitment to ethical standards, almost guarantees they will be an asset wherever they choose to work.

Chapter 3

Electronics Repairers

Every organization or company that uses electronics equipment needs access to a well-trained support staff that can set up, maintain, and repair that equipment. The military is no exception. According to the U.S. Navy's recruitment Web site, sailors with an aptitude for electronics are needed in virtually every environment in which the navy operates, both above and below the ocean: "Your skills in electronics could be the key to repairing the underwater surveillance system of a submarine operating hundreds of feet beneath the sea. Or maybe your skills with electronics will allow you to repair the laser-guidance system on an F/A-18 Hornet jet just before an important mission."[33]

All five branches of the military take full advantage of state-of-the-art technology, so they all rely heavily on electronics repairers. Though their tasks can be quite varied, the basic duties that military electronics repairers perform include installing circuits and wiring, installing computers, running diagnostic checks on equipment to identify defective components, stringing electric cables, and repairing circuits and wiring using a soldering iron. They might also monitor critical military defense systems such as radar, air traffic control, and missile tracking, to look for problems.

Because the electronics field is extremely complex, with much to learn, most military electronics repairers specialize in one type of equipment. Some learn everything there is to know about maintaining ballistic missiles and their launching systems. Others become experts at maintaining a particular aircraft's compass and navigation systems. Still others set up communications systems, ensuring that troops in the field can talk with superiors in other locations. Thus, there are ample opportunities open to high school graduates that will take full advantage of their individual interests and problem-solving skills.

Sample Specialties

There are many areas that an electronics repairer can specialize in. Depending on the military's current need, electronics repairers might train and work with fixed and mobile radio and television equipment or air traffic control equipment. Many train and work with computer and networking systems. Others specialize in fixing cryptographic equipment, navigation systems, or weapons systems. Cryptographic equipment is a crucial part of the military's secure communications system. The navy, for example, uses this equipment to encipher and decipher digital data signals between ships and land.

Electronics repairers who train and work with weapons systems conduct preventive maintenance on electronic equipment that detects, analyzes, and identifies radar emissions. For example, the repairers make sure that all of the components, such as

Electronics repairers are sometimes assigned to work in aircraft control.

fuses, are still good. Without this equipment in proper working order, the U.S. military is at a disadvantage in that it is not able to pinpoint the location, speed, and movement of enemy planes and ships. Repairers also maintain equipment that produces high-power jamming signals that thwart an enemy using radar-guided weapons systems against the U.S. military. Not all weapons systems are in a plane or on a boat; some are housed in command centers on military bases. Thus, these repairers can be found in a variety of work environments.

Electronics repairers who specialize in aviation systems also work in a variety of settings, since they are employed by every branch of the military. Much like car mechanics, they review an aircraft's electronic equipment daily to ensure that when the pilots get into the air, they can communicate, navigate, and attack enemy targets. Some of the military's aircraft cost millions of dollars apiece, so this is a highly critical role.

Some electronic instrument and equipment repairers maintain unmanned aerial vehicles (UAVs), including the U.S. Air Force's Desert Hawk. According to *Military & Aerospace Electronics* magazine, the Pentagon budgeted more than $1 million for UAV spending in 2004—and expenditures are expected to exceed $2 billion in 2005. These small planes are piloted from the ground via remote control and used primarily for aerial surveillance. The UAVs can also be used to fire weapons at targets. So the electronics repairers who are assigned to maintain the Desert Hawk must ensure that the 7-pound (3.2kg) aircraft, known officially as the Force Protection Airborne Surveillance System, is able to fly for up to an hour using rechargeable batteries and that its cameras, sensors, communications, and weapons components function properly. If any of these electrical parts cease to work or are damaged during landing, security troops on the ground lose their edge in knowing what the enemy is doing. Other electronics repairers work with other types of visual imagery and intrusion detection systems. Some, for example, maintain cameras, monitors, and videotape recorders. Others keep film processing and printing equipment in working order.

Many electronic instrument and equipment repairers specialize in communications equipment. Their job is also critical to the military's success, as troops that are deployed miles, if not conti-

Specialists in electronics work with all different types of communications equipment.

nents, from their superiors need to stay in touch during missions. Air Force Staff Sgt. Chris Hart's specialty is satellite systems equipment. He uses modems, fiber optics, and other equipment to set up field communications systems, synchronizing the communications equipment settings so the military branches can communicate with their field troops. He explains that his basic job is to ensure that signals can be sent from one location to another:

> I ensure that all of our voice and data circuits are working at 100 percent capability for the missions that go on around the world. We provide secure data, such as internet and fax and secure voice, for all of the branches of the military. We provide the means for them to coordinate. This is called "the backbone." The hardest part of our job can be making our equipment work with the other branches' equipment.[34]

Senior Airman Karl Knowlton has also trained to install communications systems. During deployment assignments, he enjoys the challenge of traveling to an unknown region, setting up needed communication equipment, and ensuring that it works "all within the first 24 hours of landing in a spot where there was nothing before."[35] Because of the inherent challenges of working in a field environment, Knowlton's skill gives him immense job satisfaction.

Necessary Skills

With so many electronics systems to maintain, the military is continually training new recruits, most of whom are recent high school graduates. Though its need for manpower is great, however, the military does not allow every recruit who expresses an interest to enter this field. Enlistees must first prove they have the necessary aptitude. Using the Armed Services Vocational

ASVAB Determines Career

Before high school graduates can work in military electronics, they must prove that they have the aptitude to do so. To determine this aptitude, the military uses the Armed Services Vocational Aptitude Battery (ASVAB), a three-hour exam that was developed by the Department of Defense. Everyone interested in joining the military must take this test.

The ASVAB is actually eight individual tests, including Word Knowledge, Paragraph Comprehension, Mathematics Knowledge, Arithmetic Reasoning, General Science, Mechanical Comprehension, Electronics Information, and Auto and Shop Information. It is the composite score from these individual tests that determines which career field(s) the recruit may enter.

High school juniors and seniors are eligible to take the high school version of the test, which is called Form 18/19. More than half of all U.S. high schools participate in ASVAB testing. Approximately nine hundred thousand students take the test each year. If the test is not available at their school, students can take the ASVAB at a military entrance processing station (MEPS) or a mobile examination team (MET) site. Students unhappy with their score can retake the test three months from the time they first took it and then every six months after that. The last test score, not the highest, is good for two years.

Aptitude Battery (ASVAB) test, the military is able to determine which enlistees possess the problem-solving skills they will need to work in electronics repair. Hart notes why this skill is important: "Sometimes a situation does not work how it is supposed to. . . . The answers to the problems are not always in the books; you have to think outside the box at times."[36]

Another factor that determines on-the-job success for electronics repairers is manual dexterity. These specialists cannot be "all thumbs." Rather, they must be good at working with their hands, as some equipment contains tiny gears, complex wiring, or sophisticated electronic controls that must be handled with care. To diagnose a problem, military electronic instrument and equipment repairers must often disassemble the small parts of a piece of equipment. Then they have to fix it, which again might require a delicate touch, before carefully putting the parts back together.

Learning the Skills

Having demonstrated the required problem-solving skills and manual dexterity, new service members assigned to be electronics repairers attend special electronics training upon completing their basic military training. During this training they learn about basic electronic theory. They also learn to work with alternating current and circuits. And they learn to conduct diagnostic checks on equipment and to repair the equipment if it is malfunctioning or broken. Since the class instruction is based on algebra, physics, and trigonometry, trainees who took these courses in high school will more quickly grasp the concepts. As well, those who took high school shop mechanics will have the advantage over trainees who have not had such previous experience. Hart found his technical training challenging, but says that it was not so hard that a high percentage of people failed out of the class:

> The instructors are more than willing to make sure you understand what you are doing before you move on to your next class. My training was nine months long and each class was from several days long to a few weeks. The job is broken down into chunks to make sure you get it piece by piece so you can put it all together for your last few classes. I think the reason that technical training was challenging

for me was because I did not have prior experience, so I had to learn it all from scratch. Several people in my class had experience in electronics so they knew how different circuits worked and how to trace out schematics in a technical order. They seemed to grasp the training quicker than most of us.[37]

Knowlton adds that the training, which is on a par with entry-level college classes, is manageable if trainees pay attention in class. Of course, they also need to study the reading material and complete the homework assignments in order to graduate. In general, classroom training varies in length between eight and forty weeks. The army conducts most of its electronics training at Fort Gordon, Georgia. The navy holds technical training in a number of locations, including Norfolk, Virginia, and Groton, Connecticut. The coast guard conducts its electronics training at ET "A" School in Petaluma, California.

Honing Advanced Skills

Electronics repairers also complete advanced individual training, specific to the type of equipment and environment in which they will be working, before being sent to their first assignment. Those assigned to work on air force communications systems, for example, take an eleven-week class in airborne communications and electronics. Since they work aboard aircraft, these repairers are also required to take a number of survival training classes. These courses include Combat Survival Training Course, Water Survival–Parachuting Course (if assigned to C-130 aircraft, which carries cargo), and Water Survival–Non-Parachuting (if assigned to aircraft other than C-130). In the combat survival course, trainees use equipment and learn techniques designed to enable them to survive in an unfriendly environment. In the parachuting course, trainees learn maneuvers that enable helicopter crews to rescue them. Though the class teaches basic skills, in the event they really do need to be rescued from an open sea environment, electronics repairers will have to deal with whatever unpredictable conditions the sea throws at them. Electronics repairers who are not comfortable in a water environment need to either mentally adjust to this environment in training or avoid enlisting with the navy.

As well, electronics repairers who enter the navy must be comfortable with confinement and small spaces if they are assigned to the navy's Submarine Electronics/Computer Field.

Tread Carefully with Recruiters

High school students who are interested in learning about a career as a military electronics repairer can contact a military recruiter to ask questions. While most recruiters provide a realistic view of the military lifestyle, some recruiters are more interested in ensuring that they make their quota, since their effectiveness is judged by the number of recruits they sign up.

Rod Powers, who maintains the military topic area on About.com, asserts that 40 percent of enlistees do not complete their initial term of service—primarily because they find their military experience to be far from their recruiter's description. While the recruiters may have stretched the truth, or even lied to sway students, some students do not listen carefully enough or simply do not ask enough questions. For instance, a recruiter might guarantee a student a slot in military electronics repair—and actually write up an enlistment contract—but the student might fail the military physical or electronics training, or fail to obtain a security clearance, and thus not get the job. Or the military might choose to assign the student elsewhere, based on staffing holes in other fields that it needs to fill.

Of the five military branches, the army, says Powers, has the worst reputation for working soldiers in jobs that have nothing to do with their Military Occupation Specialty (MOS). He adds another caution: New electronics instrument and equipment repairers may not be able to train in another field if they do not like their job—despite being told by their recruiter that they have that option. The army and air force require new recruits to serve at least thirty-six months in their original job assignment before becoming eligible for retraining—and they must usually agree to reenlist. The navy and marines require a recruit to serve at least twenty-four months in their job before applying for retraining. Unfortunately, if the preferred job is overmanned, the recruit cannot enter it.

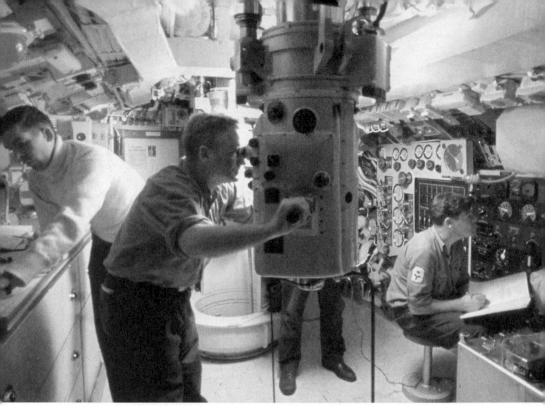

Electronic submarine systems require monitoring and maintenance. The people who do this work must go through extensive training.

Women are not allowed to serve aboard submarines, so this field is closed to them. Though a Pentagon civilian advisory panel recommended in 2000 that the navy allow women to serve aboard submarines, the navy has so far declined, claiming that the subs are too cramped to afford women privacy. The navy estimates that redesigning Virginia-class attack submarines with enough crew space to accommodate gender-integrated crews would cost an extra $4 million per submarine.

Electronics repairers who can mentally deal with a submarine environment receive extensive training in the operation and maintenance of electronic submarine systems, including combat control, sonar, navigation, and communications systems. Trainees learn about electricity, computers, digital systems, fiber optics, and electronics repair. But first they attend Basic Enlisted Submarine School (BESS) to become submarine qualified. BESS is a full month of intensive training. According to an article from Navy News Service, one exercise that trainees must successfully complete in order to graduate takes place in a replicated submarine space known as the "wet trainer." There, students must battle 20,000 gallons (75,700l) of water leaking from twelve pipes and flanges, working against quickly rising water levels to save the sub. It is not an easy task, says Seaman Recruit Joseph Drawns: "I thought everything [all the coursework] was going to be a bit slower. You had to really be on your toes."[38] Another exercise has trainees battling a room of smoke and fire—in the dark. Because instructors have only four weeks to introduce trainees to almost every system and major piece of equipment on the submarine, training is intense. Trainees spend nearly twelve hours a day in classroom instruction and study.

A high school graduate seeking an opportunity to gain a wide range of experience in electronics repair might look closely at the coast guard. Electronics repairers working in the other branches typically train for and handle just one area. But since the coast guard is significantly smaller than the other military branches, its electronics repairers do not specialize to the extent that those working in the other branches do. Thus, a coast guard electronics repairer might get to train and work in radio and satellite communications, radar, telephone, computers, and electronic warfare during his or her career.

Perils and Dangers

The perquisites or perks of working in military electronics include a high level of autonomy, responsibility, and job satisfaction. Hart explains why he enjoys working in military satellite communications: "You look around and realize that you are responsible not only for the airmen on your crew, but for millions of dollars worth of equipment. It is a lot of responsibility, but it is also a great satisfaction."[39]

Despite the perks there are some physical dangers that military electronics repairers face, whether they are assigned to a sub, ship, plane, or an office environment. The primary physical danger is the possibility of being electrocuted, especially when new repairers first start out in the career. Air Force Staff Sgt. Mark Morris explains: "There was a time when I got a nice jolt of power at least a couple of times per day. The voltage obviously was not life-threatening, but it was unpleasant just the same."[40]

Military electronics installers and repairers might also be injured by radio frequency burns, radiation, and noise pollution.

Because radiation effects are cumulative, radiation sickness can occur from repeated exposures to the small doses of electromagnetic radiation given off by electronics equipment. Repairers suffering from radiation sickness might experience blistering skin burns, hair loss, vomiting, and diarrhea. This is one reason the military so highly stresses safety on the job. Hart explains: "We have many different types of antenna systems as well and they radiate high frequencies that can harm a person. But the key thing is that the military takes many precautions to protect their

The work of electronics technicians, such as repair and routine maintenance on communications antennas, can be hazardous.

Flexible Citizenship

Unlike in some military career fields, high school graduates interested in joining the military as electronics repairers do not need to be U.S. citizens, unless their duties require a security clearance. They must, however, be legal immigrants who are permanently residing in the United States. They also must have a valid Immigration and Naturalization Service Alien Registration Card (INS Form I-151/551), commonly referred to as a green card. Their green card must remain valid throughout their enlistment period. But to extend their enlistment, which is called reenlisting, these legal immigrants must first become citizens. Because of their active duty status, they have the option of an accelerated citizenship program.

personnel. We have safety switches that disable voltages and radiations when something goes wrong."[41]

Another danger of the job is possible lifting hazards. Some of the equipment that Hart totes around weighs a couple of hundred pounds. And there is always the chance that he might fall from a ladder or tower, breaking a leg or injuring himself even more severely. Some of the antennas Hart has had to climb are 38 feet (11.6m) across. His worst climbing experience, however, was when he had to crawl up a ladder to get to a roof—during a bad rainstorm.

In case of emergencies, the military requires that its electronics personnel become CPR-certified. CPR (cardiopulmonary resuscitation) can save a person's life by restoring breathing and circulation, through a combination of rescue breathing and chest compressions, until an emergency medical team arrives.

Pay and Promotion

Since many electronics repairers enter the military upon graduating from high school, they have much to look forward to. For one thing, they can expect to receive whatever training they need to do their jobs. And under the military's strict guidelines, they can expect regular performance reviews—and with good reviews

After completing military service, electronics repairers can enter a variety of fields including repairing and testing satellite dishes.

come regular promotions and pay raises. According to the 2005 military budget, brand new E-1s receive a base salary of $1,142 per month. At six months, if promoted to an E-2, they receive a base salary of $1,384. After five years, the base salary jumps to $1,759 for E-5. At thirteen years of service, however, as E-6s, electronics repairers receive only $1,920 a month. It can be extremely difficult to raise a family on this annual salary.

Though pay is certainly one area that many electronics repairers feel could be improved, Hart notes that the other perks he receives from the military put things in balance for him:

> I worked at Hardee's [a fast food restaurant] for two years. I know what crappy pay is. Our pay is not that bad, although it could be better. If I didn't like my career, though, I wouldn't be here. And I get many benefits from the military. My family and I have [free] medical coverage, dental plans, and use of base recreation and education

facilities. The military helped pay for my bachelor's degree and it will help pay for my master's as well.[42]

Future Outlook

According to the Department of Labor, more than 100,000 service members served in the military's electronics and electronic repair fields in 2003. The navy utilized more than 52,000 electronics specialists, while the air force had more than 37,000. The army allocated more than 14,000 soldiers to this work. With only 3,530 slots, the coast guard offered the least opportunity for electronics enlistees to serve, as it is significantly smaller than the other military services, but for that very reason, its repairers have much more diversity in their duties than do those working in the other branches.

Many electronics repairers reenlist for more than one service commitment. However, should they choose to leave the military after their initial enlistment period, many military electronics repairers easily find similar jobs in the civilian sector, such as in manufacturing businesses, government agencies, communications firms, and commercial airlines. Their marketability comes from the fact that civilian companies appreciate that the military gave them ample training and instilled in them a sense of discipline. Hart believes that when he is ready to consider a civilian job, his military experience will give him a competitive edge over many civilian job hunters: "Employers know they are more than likely getting someone who can follow directions and be a leader at the same time."[43]

Some of these job seekers accept positions as computer technicians, telephone repairers, and aircraft technicians. Others work as guidance systems specialists, computer network managers, or radio and radar repairers. Some even open their own businesses. According to the U.S. Department of Labor, precision instrument and equipment repairers held 64,000 jobs in 2002, so there are many opportunities for military repairers entering the civilian work force. Regardless of the field they enter, many electronics repairers cite the military as the environment that taught them to successfully think and perform independently. These qualities are appreciated by private companies looking to hire electronics repairers.

Chapter 4

Pilots

Pilots are indispensable to the U.S. military, whether they are flying rescue missions in coast guard helicopters, dropping bombs on hostile targets from high-tech air force bombers, or conveying troops and equipment via army transport planes. The navy, armed with aircraft carriers, employs pilots to complete missions in areas where fixed runways are impossible, and the Marine Corps, which prefers to function as a self-contained unit although it is part of the navy, relies on pilots to fly its fighters, bombers, and attack helicopters. Without its superior and swift air power, the U.S. military would be severely handicapped in protecting American interests and allies.

As exemplary pilots are critical to the success of U.S. military strategy, the military puts pilot enlistees through rigorous training programs, spending hundreds of thousands of dollars on each trainee. All recruits spend many hours in training exercises to learn to handle every aspect of their aircraft. This repetition is critical, says Air Force Major Brian Hill, since "training is practice, just like for a football team. Most of our practice is in the plane, but we also do about thirty hours a year of simulator training. Our training is second to none."[44] Thanks to this education, the U.S. military can boast the world's best-trained pilots.

A Total Commitment

Though the military's pilot training is extremely difficult, the stress level only intensifies once a graduate is flying real missions. Since September 11, 2001, military pilots and their crews have been pushed to their limits, says Heather Baldwin, an air force KC-135 tanker pilot, because of longer work days and more frequent missions: "It's been difficult since 9/11. Right now we're gone on deployments more than two hundred days a year. We fly so much that people are getting tired."[45]

In addition to their hours in the cockpit, pilots also spend many hours on the ground getting ready for missions, organizing training exercises to ensure that their crews remain combat-ready, and filling out flight paperwork. A pilot's work schedule is rarely standard. Air force bomber pilot Kristin Goodwin explains:

> I don't have a nine-to-five job. I work twelve- to fourteen-hour days. I got up at 3:30 this morning, it's 8:30 P.M. now, and I'm still in my uniform. At any time I could get a call saying no more than "Be in in twelve hours." I go in, they brief me, and I'm off on my mission. But the most difficult thing for me is that I can't "just" be a pilot. We have an obligation to be leaders as well. Our additional duties are so consuming.[46]

It is important that those interested in becoming military pilots realize that the military expects total commitment from its aviators. Thus, it is a challenge for military pilots to have a full

A military pilot waits in his cockpit. Whether flying rescue missions, dropping bombs, or moving troops, pilots are invaluable to the U.S. military.

Learning to Survive

All military pilots complete Survival, Evasion, Resistance and Escape (SERE) training, to prepare for the possibility of being shot down, captured, or interrogated by the enemy. SERE teaches basic first aid and how to trap small game, to make signals, to build shelters, to navigate using a map and compass, and to travel without detection. In an interview with the author, Capt. Darisse Smith, an army helicopter pilot, summed up her SERE experience this way:

> Basically, it ends up being about five days of walking around with no food. After a while your body starts eating itself and you don't feel hungry. I lost about eight pounds. The instructors provided us with water, so it wasn't a practical exercise in survival but in interrogation. We got yelled at a lot and they tried to pit my team members against each other.

The purpose of SERE training is to push trainees to their physical and mental limits. During her SERE training, air force bomber pilot Kristin Goodwin was placed in a box so small she could not move. Though she is claustrophobic, Goodwin was able to find the mental strength to calm her fear. She believes the experience added to her ability to be a good pilot. In an interview with the author, she said, "You need to know your physical limits, as you're entrusted with high levels of information. We can't crack and give up that information. . . . I now have the confidence that I would be okay."

family life or personal life, since remaining flight-ready demands a great deal of time. Even weekends might be spent reviewing flight manuals. To find job satisfaction as a military pilot, says air force recruiter Staff Sgt. Richard Clemens, "You have to be really motivated and know that it's the most important thing to you."[47]

Before pilot trainees have the opportunity to prove their commitment, they must overcome some huge obstacles. Their desire for flying is not enough to guarantee them a spot as a military aviator. They must demonstrate technical skill and, even more important, prove that they are team players and leaders. Baldwin explains: "You wouldn't believe how many average people are flying planes. You don't have to be a rocket scientist. The biggest thing is your attitude."[48]

Physical Requirements

Despite having the proper attitude, however, many enlistees never get the chance to fly because their bodies let them down. Some fail the comprehensive military flight physical that carefully screens their body systems, including respiratory and circulatory systems. Other trainees find out they have eye conditions that have the potential to hinder their vision in high altitudes.

Since the military must ensure that minor health conditions do not become serious when aggravated by flying, trainees with eye, nose, mouth, lung, and heart problems are typically barred from training and flying. Yet even less severe medical conditions can ground trainees. The coast guard, for example, requires trainees to have clean dental exams, because cavities and teeth and gum problems can be negatively affected by changes in air pressure.

Each military branch has its own vision and fitness requirements for pilot training. The air force requires pilot trainees to have eyesight of at least 20/70, correctable to 20/20 with glasses. The navy and Marine Corps trainee requirement is more forgiving, at 20/100. To enter army helicopter flight training, or to train with the coast guard, applicants must have at least 20/50 vision, correctable to 20/20. All branches require normal depth perception and color vision. Only recently has the military allowed individuals who have had laser eye surgery before enlisting to enter flight school. This is because Lasik and other corrective eye surgeries can affect flying, including causing reduced night vision. The military does allow for vision deterioration over a pilot's career, but it does not permit pilots to continue flying if their uncorrected vision declines beyond 20/400.

The military also has established maximum age requirements for applicants, taking into consideration that today's graduates make a ten-year service commitment. The navy and marines require applicants to be between the ages of nineteen and twenty-six, although some older applicants already serving in the military might be allowed to enter the flight program if issued a special waiver. (Waivers allow the military to be flexible on a case-by-case basis.) The air force and army require applicants to enter training before turning thirty. The coast guard, which helps protect the nation only in times of conflict, does not accept applications from anyone over thirty-two years of age. Coast guard applicants must also have accrued five hundred hours as a rated pilot with another military branch. These guidelines may fluctuate with staffing levels.

College Degrees

The only military branch that does not require pilots to have a college degree is the army. For the majority of recruits then, the quickest route to military pilot training is to enter the military with a college degree. It will take considerably longer if high school graduates enlist and then work toward a degree. This is because after taking years to complete their degree part-time, enlistees must gain entry into Officer Training (if in the air force) and Office Candidate School (if in the army, navy, or Marine Corps) before applying to flight school. Goodwin cautions that this route, though certainly doable, is more difficult as enlistees "have to do exceptionally well to apply to be an officer. They have to do their job up to standard while taking their classes."[49]

Thus, a high school graduate who aspires to be a military pilot should consider applying to the Naval Academy in Annapolis, Maryland, or the Air Force Academy near Colorado Springs, Colorado. These military colleges educate and train young men and women in military knowledge and leadership skills. Students interested in aviation can take advantage of classes that help them to hone basic aviation skills.

Application to either academy requires a congressional recommendation from the high school student's state representative. Students who submit their application packets early gain the advantage, says Clemens: "I tell kids that if they haven't been working on their application by eleventh grade to hang it up. By their senior year they're well behind the curve."[50] This is because the Air Force Academy receives eighty thousand applications each year—but accepts only twelve hundred cadets.

Students can gain similar military training by securing a Reserve Officers' Training Corps (ROTC) scholarship, which are available at about one thousand colleges and universities. These scholarships require the students to participate in military training on and off their school campuses. While most of their time is spent in physical training, they also learn to follow orders, and to conduct themselves appropriately. Students can qualify for three levels of scholarship, but most scholarships go to those applicants who declare technical majors, such as engineering. All scholarship recipients receive a nontaxable monthly stipend (allowance) during the academic year. The current amount is $250 for freshmen,

Thunderbird Teamwork

The Thunderbirds, the famous U.S. Air Force Aerial Demonstration Squadron, serve as an effective marketing tool to help the air force attract new pilots to its program. The eight pilots of the Thunderbird team perform, on average, seventy times each year, wowing crowds across the country with their daring aerial maneuvers.

This hectic travel schedule keeps the pilots on the road for more than two hundred days a year. But they do not travel alone. They are supported by more than one hundred enlisted airmen whose job is to ensure that the pilots' twelve F-16 Fighting Falcon jets, in which they demonstrate the precision flying skills demanded of every air force fighter pilot, remain in peak flying condition. Together, team members showcase the air force's dedication to teamwork, safety, training, and technology.

Each pilot logs more than one thousand hours of military jet experience prior to joining the Thunderbird team. Each pilot also flies more than one hundred practice demonstrations before performing for the public. The supporting team members, who have at least three years of air force service, complete a twenty-one-day training program to learn each team member's function, the squadron's history, and daily operations. They must pass a test with a score of 80 percent or higher in order to receive their Thunderbird patch.

$300 for sophomores, $350 for juniors, and $400 for seniors. The air force scholarship requirements include U.S. citizenship, at least a 3.0 cumulative grade point average, class ranking in the top 40 percent, and an SAT composite of eleven hundred or ACT composite of twenty-four. Cadets must also pass a physical fitness test, which includes push-ups, crunches, and a one-and-a-half-mile run.

Only the army allows high school graduates to apply for pilot training, through its Warrant Officer Flight Training (WOFT) program, whose slogan is "From High School to Flight School." However, applicants who have two years of college credit, a private pilot's license, and proven leadership skills receive preference over applicants with just a high school diploma. To even be considered, students must score 90 or higher on the Army Flight Aptitude Selection Test (the maximum score is 176), earn a minimum General Technical (GT) score on the Armed Services Vocational Aptitude Battery (ASVAB) test, and pass a flight physical examination.

Choosing a Branch

Hopeful aviators may have a tough time determining which military branch is best for them. One way to do so is to evaluate how each branch would meet their long-term flying goals. The army offers students the opportunity of circumventing college, and then places its warrant officer pilots in the cockpit for the duration of their careers. Its officer pilots, however, spend less time in their aircraft as they promote to broader leadership roles. College students might choose to become warrant officers upon enlistment, then, if their interest lies more in flying than leading.

Some students may make their decision based on schooling or scholarships, or the type of flight missions each branch typically conducts. Capt. Darisse Smith says she chose the army because she liked the "down and dirty" of ground combat: "I'm an aviator, but I'm still expected to be a foot soldier, and able to dig a foxhole."[51] For others, the location of their base assignment might be the key factor. The army, for instance, tends to place its people in remote geographic locations, while navy bases are situated near water. The air force offers the nicest base perks of any branch, including gyms and nicer housing.

Air force and navy pilots fly fixed-wing aircraft like this F-14 fighter jet.

The type of aircraft that trainees hope to fly is another important consideration. The military operates two types of aircraft: fixed-wing and rotary-wing. While most air force and navy pilots fly fixed-wing aircraft, such as bombers, fighters, and cargo planes, most army and marine pilots fly helicopters, which are rotary-wing aircraft. Fixed-wing pilots fly high in the sky, while helicopter pilots fly low, usually right over the tree line. Each environment offers its own challenges. Helicopter pilots, for instance, might experience engine trouble and risk crashing, while high-altitude pilots have to deal with the physical stresses of g-forces. The term *g-force* is a way of describing the amount of pressure a jet pilot feels during steep ascents or descents. Pilots can black out from g-forces if their brain receives inadequate oxygen as blood is forced downward by gravity.

Early Prep

To gain real piloting experience, which might help them decide what types of aircraft they want to fly, high school students can join the Civil Air Patrol (CAP), a civilian voluntary organization linked to the air force. The CAP Cadet program is open to students between the ages of twelve and twenty-one. CAP offers private pilot instruction, background on the air force, and skills in search and rescue. A side benefit of joining is that CAP offers more than $300,000 in college scholarships annually—and many of the scholarships go unused.

Students can also prepare for pilot training by refining their motor skills. Participation in team sports that develop their skills in hitting, dribbling, or shooting a ball is a good place to start. Goodwin recommends that those interested in entering a flying program also develop a proficiency in visualization. She explains how she uses a mental exercise she calls "chair flying" to improve her performance:

> Your brain doesn't know if you're doing an event or just practicing an event. For instance, in preparing for a skydiving competition in college, we couldn't dive because of rain. So I sat in a chair and did ten jumps in my head. It was exhausting, but the next day when I competed I was ready.[52]

A military trainee participates in a flight simulator exercise. Students and others can use this computer software to practice take-offs, flying, and landings.

This technique has proven scientific results; one study found that muscle mass is enlarged through visualization of a repeated activity. This exercise also helps to develop a good memory, which is required of all good pilots.

Pilot Bryant Dixon adds that students who want a flying career should take math and especially physics classes where they would learn the concepts of lift and drag. Without understanding the forces that enable a plane to exceed the force of gravity and overcome the resistance of air flow as it is propelled through the air, says Dixon, students will not understand how to maintain this equilibrium: "The plane isn't particularly forgiving; it will do what you tell it to do. If you tell it to do something wrong, people might die."[53]

Students might also take advantage of software programs such as Microsoft Flight Simulator. This realistic computer program's visuals enable users to experience weather conditions, takeoffs, and landings. Because the program also reviews users' flight performance, Dixon asserts: "It is one of the best teaching tools for aspiring pilots. Going through all of the courses within the software gives students an incredible head start in future flying programs."[54]

The Challenge of Training

Having experienced simulated and real flying, new recruits can approach the military's difficult pilot training with confidence. Although there are differences in the fixed-wing and rotary-wing training programs, both revolve around intense class study, simulation training, and actual flying. For at least a year, trainees have little time for other activities in their lives. During this time, they endure the physical, emotional, and mental stress of being under constant pressure to learn and perform. To get through this period, Baldwin says she had to tell herself daily that she would not fail: "I had to decide that I was going to get through, that they weren't going to break me. I knew I could wash out if I underperformed."[55]

The training is challenging because U.S. aircraft have become highly sophisticated. In an article on the Air Force News Service Web site, an engineer with the Air Force Research Laboratory writes: "Today's cockpit is an information center. . . . The pilot has to assess a massive input of data in seconds to determine a course of action. . . . Instinct and courage are still in the equation, but pilots today also have much more information than pilots from other generations could have dreamed."[56] To acquire an ease with this barrage of information, trainees train for twelve hours a day. Instructors evaluate trainees' flying ability, attitude, written exams, and communication skills. Before getting their wings, trainees are evaluated on real flights. A trainee whose performance is inadequate might be kicked out of the flight program. Air force pilot Ryan Huckabay explains:

> Once the flying starts you spend the rest of training just a breath away from ending your flying career. Three failed flights or one failed check ride [a test that ensures pilots have gained satisfactory flight skills] could lead to a "progress check," which is another flight to see if you are a failure risk. A failed progress check leads to an "elimination check" to see if you have any potential to graduate. Fail the elimination check and you're sent to a Flight Evaluation Board that can send you back to training or kick you out of the military for life. . . . I had friends who were doing great one week and were gone the next. We started training with twenty-nine and ended with seventeen.[57]

Fixed-Wing Aircraft

Except in the army and Marine Corps, which rely mainly on helicopters, most military pilots fly fixed-wing planes. Air force trainees start out on a twin engine jet, usually the T-37B Tweet or T-6A Texan II, to learn how to read the instruments and guide the plane through turns and dives. They proceed to advanced training, but only learn the aircraft they will ultimately fly at the conclusion of training. Once all the test flights have been completed, the trainees are ranked against each other. Those with the best evaluations are given first choice in choosing the type of aircraft they want to fly. Based on their natural skills and preference for how each aircraft handles, some air force trainees jump at the opportunity to fly the B-2 Spirit Bomber or the F-117 Nighthawk stealth fighter. Bomber pilots, who possess expert flying skills and steely determination, drop weapons on enemy targets. Fighter

A military pilot rides in a crash simulator. Using simulators like this one is a crucial part of a pilot's training.

pilots fly the fastest and most powerful jet fighters in the world and frequently engage the enemy.

Pilots of both types of aircraft spend many hours reviewing mission details before they step into their cockpits. They check that they have the right coordinates, for example, and that their crews understand their mission duties. Pilot trainees who prefer to spend fewer hours in mission analysis should consider other types of aircraft, says Baldwin:

> I was stationed at a fighter base and I thought it would be cool to be a fighter pilot until I went on a mission and saw that they briefed three hours before the hour-and-a-half mission, and then debriefed for five hours! And when they're not flying they're studying. One wife told me that her husband spends three hours every Saturday morning reading his flight manual to stay current.[58]

Col. Jack Shanahan, who flew fighter planes for sixteen years before moving over to intelligence, agrees: "The most challenging aspect of the job was the time and energy it took to stay on

In-Flight Refueling

The air force airmen who perform in-flight refuelings are called boom operators or boomers. It is their job to connect a 40-foot-long (12m) telescoping boom from their aircraft to a fighter jet or other aircraft in need of fuel. Fuel is funneled through this boom from one aircraft to another. In-flight refueling is an important job: It not only allows an aircraft to continue on its mission without landing for fuel, but it also prevents excessive wear and tear on the aircraft inflicted by landings. Boomers go through fourteen weeks of training, including simulator training, to learn and practice this skill. They then complete eight flights with an instructor before moving to their assigned command. There, they complete 120 days of on-the-job training before they are allowed to fly solo. This training is important: In a single minute, boomers can pump more fuel into an aircraft than the average passenger car is able to use in a full year, and in eight minutes their planes can pump more fuel than a gas station would if it were pumping twenty-four hours a day, seven days a week for a year.

Three planes demonstrate how tankers refuel fighter jets in flight.

top of the game. It was not unusual to spend twelve hours getting ready for a flight, flying, and then talking about the mission . . . even though the flight itself was shorter than 90 minutes."[59]

Other graduates, more comfortable in larger planes, might hope for assignments with the C-135, a supertanker. Tanker pilots transport fuel to other planes for in-flight refueling. Each C-135 is operated by a three-person crew: the pilot, copilot, and boom operator (refueler). The pilots ensure that the tanker is properly inspected, loaded, equipped, and manned before each mission. For each mission, tanker pilots must figure out how much gas they need to transport, how weather conditions may affect the success of the mission, and what training requirements the crew must meet in order to be ready to fly. The pilot's challenge is that these variables are always different with each mission.

While the air force program is completed in a year, navy pilots do not earn their "wings of gold" until they have spent eighteen to twenty-four months studying aerodynamics, aircraft engine systems, meteorology, navigation, flight planning, and aircraft safety. Navy Naval Flight Officers gain their wings in twelve to eighteen months. Both are assigned to their first squadron after six to nine months of aircraft-specific training that includes air-to-air combat, bombing, search and rescue, landing and taking off on aircraft carriers, over-water navigation, and low-level flying.

Marine pilots, having graduated from the Naval Aviation School, fly high-speed, sophisticated aircraft such as the F/A-18D Hornet jet and giant transport planes such as the Hercules. The marines are the only branch to use the AV-8B Harrier II jet, which can take off and land vertically for attack and destroy and escort missions. Because it is equipped to be refueled while flying, the Marine Corps can deploy it for extended operations without having to worry about landing sites.

Opting for Rotary-Winged Aircraft

Yet the military also relies heavily on its rotary-winged aircraft, or helicopters, which pilots must land to refuel. Helicopters are critical to the army and Marine Corps because they are used to transport troops and supplies. All army aviators receive helicopter training. The army's aviation branch is critical to the success of army operations, since aircraft are used in combat and to haul troops and supplies. Army pilots learn to fly helicopters by study-ing flight physics, flight systems, emergency procedures, flight map reading, flight map drawing, and combat maneuvers. Graduates can fly any of the army's rotary-winged aircraft, includ-ing the RC-7, a reconnaissance and surveillance aircraft, and the C-12, a VIP (very important person) staff transport helicopter.

A platoon leader, Darisse Smith pilots the OH-58D Kiowa Warrior helicopter, which the army uses to conduct reconnais-sance missions. She says it was only through repeated simulated engine failures—and a lot of bumpy landings—that she gained the confidence to handle any emergencies that could come up during actual missions. Smith describes a typical training mission in her Kiowa, which has the capability of firing rockets and missiles:

> Last week we were working with an infantry company. We went ahead of them and reconned the route they were tak-ing and calling back if we saw any enemy on the road. Usually I'd be calling up to my higher up and consolidating

Soldiers disembark an army helicopter. Pilots who fly helicopters like this one make an important contribution to the U.S. military.

what I'm seeing with what my other aircraft are seeing. There are four radios in my aircraft, so it does get busy and difficult to manage. But you typically split your radio responsibility with the other crew. You need to listen to all of it, but focus in on what you're responsible for.[60]

Navy graduates might also be assigned to a rotary-winged aircraft, such as the SH-60 Seahawk helicopter. This is the perfect cockpit for the pilot who enjoys the thrill of flying close to the ocean waves in search of enemy submarines and underwater mines.

Salary and Benefits

Pilots are some of the most respected members of the military, due to their flying skill, leadership skills, and their willingness to fly into dangerous combat zones. The military rewards this commitment with annual bonuses, which are a nice addition to a pilot's base pay. Those flying the Apache, for instance, can get bonuses of up to $12,000 a year. However, bonus pay fluctuates yearly, depending on the military's need for pilots. In recent years Congress increased combat pay from $150 per month to $225 per month, for military members assigned to or deployed to a combat zone, which is added to their monthly base pay. However, base pay becomes significant only after climbing the ranks. O-3s (captain), for example, are paid a base monthly salary of at least $3,124. O-5s (lieutenant colonel) receive a base monthly salary of $4,118. As full colonels (O-6), officers receive a base pay of at least $4,940. Shanahan is quick to point out that there are many benefits to staying in a long-term military pilot career:

> Nobody joins the military to get rich, but as an aviator I get paid extremely well; the money was not great for the first twelve to fourteen years, but once you become a lt. colonel or colonel and you get flying pay, it's impossible to complain about money. Every time a friend gets out of the military, I get to hear about all the benefits they miss. The grass is always greener on the other side, but I haven't heard too many people brag about the great benefits they get in their civilian jobs—especially when it comes to federal and state taxes.[61]

Future Outlook

There are about twenty thousand fixed-wing pilots and sixty-five hundred helicopter pilots in the military. With the increase in global terrorism, this field is expected to grow. Pilots enjoy some of the best financial perks the military offers, but for those who decide to leave before retirement, many civilian jobs are available, including piloting for commercial airlines and private companies and teaching as flight instructors. In some areas of the country, veteran military pilots might even find jobs as crop dusters. Wherever they choose to work, pilots bring with them a high level of training and experience, and private companies are quick to recognize and take advantage of these skills.

Chapter 5

Special Forces

When the U.S. military needs to conduct specialized missions, it sends in one of its elite special forces. Around the globe, these highly trained men are involved in clandestine operations that involve rescue, combat, or teaching friendly foreign forces how to conduct war. In his book *America's Special Forces*, David Bohrer writes: "Special operators do the deeds that no one else dares. . . . They sneak behind enemy lines, assault well-defended enemy military bases and airfields, and rescue soldiers and hostages. They are called upon when diplomacy fails and political or military considerations rule out the deployment of a larger conventional force."[62]

Technically, *Special Forces* refers only to the army's Green Berets. The elite forces of the other military branches are properly called Special Operations Forces, known as Special Ops. But all are special, as these men have proven they have the skills to get the job done. Women do not have the option of participating in Special Forces. Congress and the Secretary of Defense excluded them in 1994, on the basis that special ops members have direct ground combat with the enemy.

Special forces require exceptional physical fitness, yet it is mental toughness that ultimately drives mission success. Each special ops member must willingly embrace danger, pushing his body to the extreme to overcome obstacles that stand in his way. One special ops member shares his philosophy: "I won't let anything beat me. There is nothing that I can't do. It may seem arrogant, but it's the way I think. The harder the challenge, the better."[63]

The Right Man for the Job

There is no "best" special force, as each branch has areas of expertise. This means that applicants will be able to find a place that best utilizes their particular skills and interests. The army's special forces, for example, conduct offensive raids, demolitions, intelligence, and search and rescue missions. Navy SEALs use the ocean to covertly slip in and out of enemy territory, or they act as decoys to confuse the enemy. And air force pararescuemen conduct rescue missions of people and materials in every corner of the world and in every type of environment.

The Army's Distinct Three

The army provides a wide range of opportunities in its three special forces: the Rangers, the Green Berets, and Delta Force. Rangers, identified by their tan berets, are considered the finest light infantry force in the world. They parachute into the middle of a war zone, perform strikes and ambushes, and capture enemy airfields. It was the Rangers that helped to rescue Private Jessica Lynch, who was wounded and captured in 2003, from an Iraqi hospital. Recruited only from airborne-qualified army soldiers, Rangers are trained to operate on any terrain, in any climate. They fully dedicate themselves to completing the mission—even if they have to crawl to their target.

The army's Green Berets are known for their intellectual approach. According to an article in *Newsweek*,

> Green Berets . . . tend to go into a hostile situation with more brains than brawn. Their combat training is every bit as physically grueling as the Rangers'—and they can and will fight if they need to—but Green Berets spend as much time, if not more, learning foreign languages and immersing themselves in the history and culture of far-flung regions they are assigned to. A Ranger might be awakened in the middle of the night to march 20 miles [32km] in a swamp. A Green Beret would be roused out of bed and ordered to draw a freehand map of a country selected at random, labeling every city, river and mountain range.[64]

Green Berets gather intelligence and raid behind enemy lines. They approach their targets by land, sea, or air, using canoes, small boats, motorcycles, and all-terrain vehicles. When approaching from the sky, they use steerable parachutes that guar-

A navy SEAL waits for orders. SEALs are one branch of the U.S. military's Special Forces.

antee precise landings. Going unnoticed during missions is critical, so Green Berets organize in teams called A-Teams. The teams include two weapons sergeants, two communications sergeants, two medical sergeants, and two engineering sergeants.

Delta Force, a superelite counterterrorist force, is the army's smallest special ops group. Since 1977, Delta Force has operated as a hostage-rescue force. Because it is the most covert of the U.S. Military Special Operations Forces, nearly every aspect of Delta is highly classified, including its training program and organizational structure.

The Navy and Marines

The navy has named its special forces unit after the environments in which it operates, the *sea, air,* and *land*. In their element in the water, SEALs conduct surveys of foreign seas and rivers at landing zones, clear underwater mines or other obstacles prior to amphibious landings, and salvage submerged aircraft and ships. SEALs also effectively conduct land missions. SEALs were so effective, in fact, against Vietnamese Communist guerrillas in the 1960s that the Vietcong called them "devils with green faces," in reference to their camouflage. During the 1991 Gulf War, SEALs conducted false amphibious landings to confuse and divert Iraqi forces. And in 2002, SEALs searched seventy caves in Afghanistan looking for Osama bin Laden, the terrorist behind the attack on the United States on September 11, 2001. What was supposed to be a twelve-hour search turned into an eight-day mission.

The Marine Corps also has special forces, but its two groups were not formed until 2003. The Corps considers all its "Leathernecks" tough and combat-ready, so it was reluctant to designate any of its units as elite. But after watching special ops missions funnel to the other branches, it decided to form Force Recon and Detachment One. Force Recon members are usually the first marines to go into an area. In these high-risk environments, they collect intelligence and report it via satellite communications. Detachment One, an elite group of eighty-six handpicked marine and navy corpsmen, conducts ground reconnaissance support for joint military service operations.

Force Recon marines scout an area. These are usually the first soldiers to go into an enemy zone.

The Air Force's Triple Threat

The air force has three distinct special ops positions: combat controller, pararescue, and combat weatherman. These men are highly skilled in parachuting, small-unit combat, and amphibious operations. Fewer than five hundred officers and enlisted men, identified by their scarlet berets, serve as combat controllers. With their motto of "First there," they deploy quickly by land, sea, or air into hostile territory to set up landing strips and guide in helicopters and fixed-wing aircraft—without a tower or large communications system. Combat controllers are certified air traffic controllers. They conduct surveillance of potential assault zones and target areas and report on current battlefield status. They also provide limited weather observations, including surface and altitude wind data, temperature, and cloud heights.

Air force pararescuemen, known as PJs, have a motto: "That others may live." They treat, stabilize, and evacuate injured personnel, often in hostile environments. They also provide rescue and recovery assistance associated with aircraft accidents, disaster relief, and humanitarian evacuation. Sometimes they provide landing site support for National Aeronautics and Space Administration missions. Without their commitment, thousands of military members and civilians would be lost. Notes Staff Sgt. Tan Sirisak: "We respond when and where other emergency personnel can't. We are nationally-licensed paramedics and are trained in freefall [parachuting], scuba and the highest level of combat. Basically, we are a Jack-of-all-trades organization. . . . At the end of the day, we've accomplished our mission if we've saved a life."[65]

Combat weathermen, in their gray berets, are weather forecasters who have combat training. They gather and interpret local weather information and solar and lunar data and generate forecasts in support of global special operations. They are the experts who provide weather information for the U.S. troops preparing to deploy on missions.

Joining the Ranks

Currently there is a shortage of special ops members, so the military (with the exception of the Marine Corps) invites male high school graduates to apply upon enlistment. Applicants must be

SEAL Leap Frogs

One way that the navy grabs the interest of new recruits is with its Leap Frogs, a parachute team made up of fifteen navy SEALs. Sixteen million people might watch them perform at air shows and other events each season. The Leap Frogs jump from 12,500 feet (3,750m), at speeds up to 180 miles (288km) an hour, to showcase their skill, dedication, and professionalism. Leap Frogs perform precise and complex formations with their parachute canopies. In one formation, called the quad-by-side, four Leap Frogs are tethered together.

In their thirty-five-year history, the team has had a remarkable safety record, although injuries do sometimes occur. To ensure this competence, SEALs make at least two hundred jumps before joining the team. Members serve with the Leap Frog team for a three-year tour before returning to operational SEAL teams.

U.S. citizens and at least eighteen years old. They must have eyesight correctable to 20/20, normal color vision and night vision, and excellent hand-eye coordination.

In the navy's SEAL Challenge program, applicants must pass a physical fitness screening that includes swimming 500 yards (457m) in under thirteen minutes, completing forty-two push-ups in two minutes, fifty sit-ups in two minutes, and a 1.5-mile (2.4km) run in boots and long pants in under twelve minutes. Trainees are given three chances to pass the test while in boot camp. Similarly, the army's 18X (Special Forces) Enlistment Program requires recruits to score a minimum of 229 points on the Army Physical Fitness Test. The air force also has a physical screening tool, the Physical Aptitude Stamina Test.

Because the military demands high standards of its elite forces, applicants are exhaustively screened. Author Hugh McManners explains that evaluators seek to weed out anyone who easily cracks under pressure or puts himself before the good of the team:

[The special forces] are interested in individuals who can complete their mission—despite obstacles, disasters, or broken bones—even if he is the only remaining member of the team. To get someone to recognize they possess this toughness, however, is another aspect of the rigorous selection and training process. Those who seem the toughest physically may be the ones who crack the quickest under psychological pressure.[66]

Recruits train for a physical fitness exam. Special Forces applicants are required to be in top physical condition.

Transforming Troops

In passing these early tests, trainees get a taste of the physical and mental challenges to come. They must learn to function with little or no sleep or food, to expertly handle sophisticated equipment and maneuvers, and to adapt to any environment—whether the gusting winds of a snow-covered mountain or the desert's soaring temperatures. They also must learn to parachute from planes at 20,000 feet (6,100m) to approach enemy shores undetected, after swimming for miles through the ocean, and to neutralize enemy troops through deadly yet silent combat. Training provides the environment; they must bring the desire and discipline.

Only after gaining these skills do they earn the nickname "the quiet professionals." Special ops members are the antithesis of Rambo, the movie character who wreaks havoc with explosives and automatic weapons. Sgt. Aaron Switzer explains:

When you see Rambo, you see muscles and violence. Although we must be in outstanding physical shape to face endurance, we don't want to draw attention to ourselves. We're trained how to fire a weapon, but my primary weapon is my radio. If it comes down to me firing my weapon, I've screwed up or my team screwed up. Our job is too complex; we're too highly trained to be a casualty.[67]

Ongoing Training a Given

Training is a constant for any special ops member. For example, army recruits train at the John F. Kennedy Special Warfare Center and School in North Carolina. The training may take up to two years of intensive coursework. Each year, nearly eighteen hundred recruits attend the Special Forces Assessment and Selection program. For twenty-three days, evaluators judge each trainee's intelligence, physical fitness, motivation, trustworthiness, accountability, maturity, stability, judgment, decisiveness, teamwork, influence, and communications abilities. On average, only 50 percent of each class continues on to the Special Forces Qualification Course, which is twenty-four to fifty-seven weeks of intense training.

Arguably, it is the navy SEAL who endures the toughest military training. It takes more than thirty months to train a navy

SEAL to be mission-ready. Trainees learn what they are made of during the twenty-six weeks of Basic Underwater Demolition/ SEAL (BUD/S) training at the Naval Special Warfare Center in Coronado, California. In one exercise, Underwater Acclimation, candidates are thrown into a swimming pool with their ankles and wrists bound. Despite the difficulty of not having the use of their feet and hands, they must stay afloat for twenty minutes. If they pass the test, they face five grueling days known as Hell Week. In this week-long outdoor exercise trainees learn the importance of teamwork—and what it means to be a SEAL. Allowed only a total of four hours of sleep, trainees face exhausting physical exercises, including carrying their rubber boats over their heads and crawling through mud. They teeter on the brink of hypothermia, abnormally low body temperature. This is when most trainees drop out.

Navy SEALs participate in an underwater training exercise. SEALs endure a tough training regimen.

SEALs run with a log during Hell Week, a five-day long outdoor training session in which recruits are pushed to test their physical limits.

A BUD/S instructor notes that the training, though brutal, builds amazing mental strength—a skill the SEALs must hone in order to complete their missions successfully: "The belief that BUD/S is about physical strength is a common misconception. Actually, it's 90 percent mental and 10 percent physical. [Students] just decide that they are too cold, too sandy, too sore or too wet to go on. It's their minds that give up on them, not their bodies."[68] Because BUD/S training pushes recruits to their physical and mental limits, only 30 percent succeed. Each phase of running, swimming, and obstacle courses becomes increasingly difficult to complete. But more challenge lies ahead.

If they pass BUD/S, trainees must struggle through three weeks of basic airborne training, where they learn to parachute, and thirteen weeks of Swimmer Delivery Vehicle (SDV) training. These vehicles are small, battery-powered wet submersibles. Their final challenge, writes a reporter for the Air Force News Service, awaits them on the frigid mountains of Kodiak, Alaska. In near-arctic conditions, trainees must break through ice-encrusted waters, jump in without the protection of their dry suit, tread water for three to four minutes, and still be able to pull themselves out of the water. After they complete all their courses, graduates are assigned to a SEAL team and awarded the SEAL Trident pin.

A Mental Game

The air force combat controller training is also tough, taking some trainees two years to complete. Trainees are first thrust into a ten-week pararescue and combat control indoctrination course. Senior Airman Todd Popovich's class started with seventy-six students. Only eleven finished. Popovich says that the most challenging part was Motivation Week, which, similar to the SEAL training, is a three-day test of mental endurance. Popovich admits he cried like a baby after finishing it. Trainees then attend Air Traffic Control School to learn about military air regulations,

SEAL Equipment Crucial to Success

Like professionals in any other field, SEALs can do their jobs only if they have the right tools. When in water environments, SEALs use diving masks, fins, attack boards, and the Dragger LarV—a special breathing apparatus that allows each diver to rebreathe his expended air. This prevents their air bubbles from rising to the water's surface and alerting the enemy to their presence. To get ashore without detection, SEALs might approach a landing site via a Swimmer Delivery Vehicle (SDV), which can carry six SEALs in flooded (water-filled) compartments, or the Advanced SEAL Delivery System (ASDS), a minisub with two crew members, which can carry sixteen SEALs in a dry environment. In calm waters, SEALs might also use kayaks, which are versatile and not easily detected.

In arctic conditions, SEALs take advantage of equipment that helps them withstand the frigid temperatures. Their clothing, worn in layers, wicks perspiration away during strenuous activities and insulates them when they are idle so that hypothermia does not set in. Their mountaineering gear includes tow sleds, carabiners, an ice pick, snow shoes, maps, a compass, a medical kit, sleeping and cooking gear, emergency rations, grenades, and weapons.

communications, infiltration, and demolition techniques. Pararescue trainees spend a year learning in eight separate schools to become fully qualified emergency medical technicians who are also combat-ready.

Marine Force Recon trainees also go through indoctrination. One particularly grueling task is a ten-mile (16 km) run with a 50-pound (22.5 kg) rucksack on their back. Says one graduate: "It's one day of pain. It's about taking yourself beyond the limit and pushing the envelope. . . . I didn't realize it until the end, but I had been hallucinating and eating grass."[69] Many applicants do not pass the Recon course until their fifth try. But once they do, they attend the Basic Reconnaissance Course, the start of nearly nonstop training, including Airborne School, the Marine Combatant Diver School, and Survival, Evasion, Resistance and Escape (SERE) School. SERE teaches trainees how to resist interrogation if captured, and how to escape.

Honing a Specialty

Army special ops members train for a specialty role, such as weapons sergeant, medical sergeant, or communications sergeant. Those who train as weapons sergeants become specialists on all U.S. and foreign light weapons. Their new skills enable them to slip behind enemy lines to recruit, train, and equip friendly forces for guerrilla raids, clear minefields on land and under water, carry out demolition raids against enemy military targets, and select weapons placements and sites.

The medical sergeant's training, which is fifty-seven weeks long, includes advanced medical and surgical procedures. This training includes four weeks on an ambulance crew in cities with high trauma rates, such as New York City. Graduates are considered the finest first-response/trauma medical technicians in the world. They competently provide basic primary care for their special ops team for up to seven days and can sustain a combat casualty for up to seventy-two hours after an injury. They stabilize snakebites, bullet wounds, and fevers and even set broken bones. They also have a working knowledge of dentistry, veterinary care, public sanitation, water quality, and optometry.

In their thirty-two weeks of training, communications sergeants learn to install and operate special forces communications

Trainees practice infiltrating an enemy beach as part of the Special Forces underwater training.

gear, including a special message system called the Emergency Fall-Back System. They become experts in Morse code and in setting up and maintaining basic computers and radio systems. They learn to build antennas and to decode encrypted satellite communications messages that provide updated mission information.

Triple Threat

Most special ops members are qualified divers, parachutists, and endurance runners. At the Special Forces Underwater Operations School in Key West, Florida, army, navy, and air force instructors teach trainees to infiltrate enemy areas underwater without detection. The students learn about open-circuit (compressed air) scuba operations and how to use stealth to enter and exit a target area. They also learn how to use small submarines that might convey them near an enemy site.

Military free fall, considered one of the military's most demanding and potentially hazardous advanced skills, enables special ops members to use parachute operations to infiltrate enemy areas, under darkness to avoid detection. This training is held at the U.S. Army Military Free Fall Parachutist School, a five-week course taught at Fort Bragg, North Carolina, and Yuma Proving Grounds, Arizona. Trainees learn aerial maneuvers and parachute opening procedures. They complete at least thirty jumps in combat gear. Some are night jumps; others are

Glimpse into the Academy

Some high school students with an interest in joining the special forces might apply to the Air Force Academy, which is the air force's elite college. This challenging environment prepares them for military life and enables them to begin honing the leadership skills they will need to be a member of the special forces. Academy life is very structured and requires cadets to give 100 percent, as does enlistment in special forces. The Air Force Academy Web site, at www. academyadmissions.com/cadetlife/dailylife, offers a snapshot of cadet life:

As a cadet, you'll have four 50-minute periods each morning and three each afternoon. Many cadets choose to take on additional academic instruction after classes or during other unscheduled times. Breakfast and lunch are mandatory formations and after classes you'll participate in mandatory athletic activities. Unless you're an intercollegiate athlete, you'll play on an intramural team two afternoons a week, after classes. The other three afternoons you have squadron activities or discretionary time. Intercollegiate athletes usually practice or compete every afternoon and frequently on weekends, too. You'll spend many evenings studying in your room or in the library— and unless you have special permission to study late, you must be in your room and in bed at taps (the last bugle call before lights out). You will often spend Saturday mornings studying or attending parades and inspections, but will usually be free Saturday afternoons and Sundays. Your fall and spring semesters last 17 weeks each and the summer term lasts 10 weeks. Instead of a three-month summer break, you'll have three weeks.

high-altitude jumps that require oxygen and special equipment to ensure that the chute opens even if the jumper blacks out from the thin air.

Army Rangers who make it through jump school can apply for the intensive Ranger School. There, they master rock and mountain climbing while wearing full gear, boots, and heavy packs. They learn to "fast rope" from helicopters onto land and into water by sliding down a special rope using a seat harness. And they find their way back to base from deep wilderness without the aid of maps—on three hours of sleep and just enough food and water to stay alive. Only one-third graduate from training. Bohrer explains why the two-month leadership course is brutal:

> To successfully complete Ranger school, trainees must pass a total of 12 tests that range from the Army physical training test and the Ranger obstacle course, to rappelling in severe weather, an 8-mile march with a 70-pound pack, and a knot test. Students who fail to pass the tests may not sign up for Ranger school again. But those who are injured or fall ill, or who are dropped because they do not pass the classroom, exercise performance, or peer review portions of the school may try again.[70]

Individuals who fail any of their special ops training courses, and most do, are reassigned to an infantry unit. If trainees fail to qualify for a secret clearance, they are likewise barred from joining special ops. But those applicants who successfully meet all requirements begin fulfilling the U.S. Army Special Forces motto, *De Oppresso Liber*, which means "To Free the Oppressed."

Special Pay

According to the 2005 military pay scale, special ops members who are E-4s receive at least $1,162 per month. As E-6s they receive at least $1,920 per month, and E-9s earn at least $3,901 per month. But that is just the start of their monetary compensation. Because their duties are so hazardous, special ops members receive additional special pay every month, including $175 for jumps, $225 for scuba diving, and $375 for special duty pay. Pararescuemen earn $150 to $250 a month for flight pay (based on flying time); special operations combat weathermen get $300 special duty pay when on an operation. Every month Navy SEALs earn up to $175 dive pay, $300 SDV pay, $225 jump pay, $110 special duty assignment pay, and $50 to $100 for second-language proficiency.

Future Outlook

Approximately fifty-five hundred enlisted men and twenty-five hundred officers have volunteered to serve in today's military's special forces. As the military will always need elite forces that it can deploy within hours, special forces is a solid career choice, although a difficult one to enter. There are many reasons why men join special ops. Some want to serve their country; others are addicted to the challenge of pushing themselves to extremes. Others simply like the camaraderie. Special ops members grow to view each other as family because they spend so much time together. Still others find this career choice the perfect way to make a stand against evil in the world. Because of the pay, training, and sense of satisfaction they receive, many in special ops stay with the military until retirement.

The Department of Defense recently approved a retention incentive package aimed at enticing special ops members to reenlist. As a result, those in the ranks of E-4 to E-9 receive an additional $375 per month, while enlisted members and warrant officers with more than twenty-five years of service receive $750 per month. More impressive is the Critical Skills Retention Bonus offered to warrant officers and senior enlisted service members in pay grades E-6 to E-9. In addition to their base pay, they receive $150,000 for renewing for six years, $75,000 for five years, $50,000 for four years, $30,000 for three years, $18,000 for two years and $8,000 for one year. Lt. Colonel Alex Findlay explains the military's reasoning: "Our investment in these professionals is great, and the experience gained through years of service makes them invaluable assets to our nation's defense. Younger replacements can be trained, but experience is irreplaceable in the current worldwide war on terrorism."[71]

If members of special ops choose to leave the military, however, their training in scuba diving, weapons, and explosives qualifies them for special police jobs, including bomb disposal specialist and diver. Some work as personal fitness trainers and celebrity bodyguards. Others take advantage of their well-honed leadership skills and become CEOs of businesses. As these men can handle anything, however, they may find it difficult to pick a civilian career that can offer the same challenge as special ops.

Notes

Introduction: Building a Career in the Military

1. David Best, "Consider Staying in the Active Army," VetJobs.com. http://63.243.14.115/military.htm.

2. TodaysMilitary.com, "Discussion #3: Employers' Views on Veterans." www.todaysmilitary.com/discstarters/views_vets.pdf.

Chapter 1: Intelligence Specialists

3. White House, "President Addresses the Nation." www.whitehouse.gov/news/releases/2003/09/20030907-1.html.

4. Don Stauffer, "Electronic Warfare: Battles Without Bloodshed," *Futurist*, January 2000, p. 23.

5. Bruce Berkowitz, *The New Face of War: How War Will Be Fought in the 21st Century*. New York: Free Press, 2003, p. 21.

6. George Melliza, e-mail interview with author, October 2004.

7. Mary Bechdel, e-mail interview with author, October 2004.

8. Jack Shanahan, phone interview with author, October 2004.

9. Bechdel, e-mail interview.

10. Bechdel, e-mail interview.

11. Brian Garino, e-mail interview with author, October 2004.

12. Justin Calvaruzo, e-mail interview with author, October 2004.

13. Shanahan, e-mail interview.

14. Garino, e-mail interview.

Chapter 2: Security Forces

15. Christopher Castaneda, e-mail interview with author, November 2004.

16. Quoted in Danielle Burrows and Tim Barela, "Surviving Terrorism," *Airman*, September 2002. www.af.mil/news/air man/0902/consumer.html.

17. Castaneda, e-mail interview.

18. Michael Smith, phone interview with author, October 2004.

19. Michael Smith, phone interview.

20. Quoted in Jason Tudor, "Air Force Countersnipers: Eyeing the Sights," *Airman*. http://usmilitary.about.com/library/milinfo/milarticles/blafsnipers.htm.

21. Air Force News Service, "Air Force Snipers in Iraq," August 6, 2003. http://usmilitary.about.com/cs/airforce/a/afsniper2.htm.

22. Quoted in Robert Valdes, "How Military Snipers Work," HowStuffWorks.com. http://science.howstuffworks.com/sniper.htm.

23. Quoted in Robert Valdes, "How Military Snipers Work."

24. Quoted in Pat McKenna, "Quoth the Ravens, 'Nevermore,'" *Airman*, November 1997. www.af.mil/news/air man/1197/raven2.htm.

25. Derek Orling, e-mail interview with author, October 2004.

26. Orling, e-mail interview.

27. Brian Curtis, e-mail interview with author, October 2004.

28. Quoted in Kelly Luster, "Army Military Police (MPs) Deployed," Army News Service, February 16, 2004. http://usmilitary.about.com/cs/army/a/ardeployedmp.htm.

29. Castaneda, e-mail interview.

30. Curtis, e-mail interview.

31. Orling, e-mail interview.

32. William Smith, e-mail interview.

Chapter 3: Electronics Repairers

33. Navy.com, "Careers: Electronics." www.navy.com/enlisted/electronics.

34. Chris Hart, e-mail interview with author, October 2004.

35. Karl Knowlton, e-mail interview with author, October 2004.

36. Hart, e-mail interview.

37. Hart, phone interview with author, October 2004.

38. Quoted in Navy News Service, "Basic Enlisted Submarine School (BESS)." http://usmilitary.about.com/od/navytrng/a/bess.htm?terms=military+navy+electronics+training+.

39. Hart, phone interview.

40. Mark Morris, e-mail interview with author, October 2004.

41. Hart, e-mail interview.

42. Hart, phone interview.

43. Hart, phone interview.

Chapter 4: Pilots

44. Brian Hill, phone interview with author, October 2004.

45. Heather Baldwin, phone interview with author, October 2004.

46. Kristin Goodwin, phone interview with author, October 2004.

47. Richard Clemens, phone interview with author, October 2004.

48. Baldwin, phone interview.

49. Goodwin, phone interview.

50. Clemens, phone interview.

51. Darisse Smith, phone interview with author, October 2004.

52. Goodwin, phone interview.

53. Bryant Dixon, phone interview with author, October 2004.

54. Dixon, phone interview.

55. Baldwin, phone interview.

56. Quoted in Mark Kinkade, "The Future of Flight," Air Force News Service, January 2004. http://usmilitary.about.com/cs/weapons/a/futureflight.htm.

57. Ryan Huckabay, phone interview with author, October 2004.

58. Baldwin, phone interview.

59. Shanahan, phone interview.

60. Darisse Smith, phone interview.

61. Shanahan, phone interview.

Chapter 5: Special Forces

62. David Bohrer, *America's Special Forces: Weapons, Missions, Training*. St. Paul, MN: MBI, 2002, p. 8.

63. Anonymous special forces sergeant, e-mail interview with author, November 2004.

64. Pat Wingert, Donatella Lorch, and Andrew Murr, "The War of the Night: Special Forces Open the Ground War. The Making of Elite Fighters—and the Battle They Face," *Newsweek*, October 29, 2001, p. 22.

65. Quoted in *Airman*, "No Wimps Allowed," 2000. www.specialoperations.com/Schools/AFSOC/Airman_Magazine.htm.

66. Hugh McManners, *Ultimate Special Forces*. New York: DK Publishing, 2003, p. 18.

67. Aaron Switzer, phone interview with author, October 2004.

68. "U.S. Military: SEAL Training Hell Week," p. 1. http://usmilitary.about.com/od/navytrng/a/sealhellweek.htm.

69. Quoted in Jake Boerhave, "Marine Recon," *Profile*, April 2003, p. 16. www.spear.navy.mil/profile/April2003.pdf.

70. Bohrer, *America's Special Forces*, p. 48.

71. Quoted in Navy News Service, "Retention Incentive Pays for Special Operations Forces," February 2005. http://usmilitary.about.com/od/militarypay/a/specoppay.htm.

Organizations to Contact

Air Force Association (AFA)
1501 Lee Highway
Arlington, VA 22209-1198
Phone: (800) 727-3337
www.afa.org

The AFA educates the public about the critical role of aerospace power in the defense of America and supports the United States Air Force members and their families.

American Legion
700 North Pennsylvania St.
P.O. Box 1055
Indianapolis, IN 46206
Phone: (317) 630-1200
www.legion.org

Chartered by Congress in 1919 as a patriotic, war-time veterans organization, this community-service organization now numbers nearly 3 million members in nearly 15,000 American Legion Posts around the world.

Association of the U.S. Army (AUSA)
2425 Wilson Blvd.
Arlington, VA 22201
Phone: (800) 336-4570
www.ausa.org

AUSA is a private, non-profit educational organization that supports America's army, including active, National Guard, reserve, civilians, retirees and family members.

National Military Family Association (NMFA)
2500 North Van Dorn St., Suite 102
Alexandria, VA 22302-1601
Phone: (800) 260.0218
www.nmfa.org

This organization seeks to promote and protect the interests of military families by influencing the development and implementation of legislation and policies affecting them.

U.S. Department of Veterans Affairs (VA)
810 Vermont Ave. NW
Washington , DC 20420
Phone: (800) 827-1000
www.va.gov

The Department of Veterans Affairs strives to meet the needs of America's veterans and their families, in recognition of their military service to the nation.

For Further Reading

Books

ASVAB: Complete Preparation Guide: Armed Services Vocational Aptitude Battery, 2nd Ed. New York: Learning Express, 2000. In-depth information on the aptitude test required of anyone interested in military service. Includes practice tests.

Hans Halberstadt, *U.S. Marine Corps* (The Power Series). Osceola, WI: Motorbooks, 1993. Though dated, this book contains interesting information on how marine operations are designed and executed, the making of a marine, and the history of the Marine Corps.

Boone Nicolls, *Airman's Guide*, 6th rev. ed. Mechanicsburg, PA: Stackpole, 2004. This text has been newly revised to include the latest information needed by airmen and noncommissioned officers for successful duty in the air force.

Scott Ostrow, *Guide to Joining the Military.* Lawrenceville, NJ: ARCO, 2000. An excellent resource that helps people figure out if a military career is suitable for them. Information on interacting with military recruiters, taking the Armed Services Vocational Aptitude Battery (ASVAB) exam, and surviving military basic training.

Raquel D. Thiebes, *Army Basic Training: Be Smart, Be Ready.* Philadelphia: Xlibris, 2001. An insider's view of army basic training.

Web Sites

About.com's U.S. Military Topic Area (http://usmilitary.about.com). A very comprehensive online resource of military career information.

Air Force Recruitment Site (www.airforce.com). Basic information on the U.S. Air Force experience, including careers and training.

Army Recruitment Site (www.goarmy.com). Full army recruitment information.

Civil Air Patrol (www.cap.gov). A student organization that teaches basic flight skills.

Coast Guard Recruitment Site (www.uscg.mil/jobs). Site offers important information to read before applying to the coast guard.

Marine Corps Recruitment Site (www.marines.com). A wealth of information for the person interested in enlisting in the Marine Corps.

Microsoft Flight Simulator (www.microsoft.com/games/flight simulator). Computer software program that helps users learn and improve their piloting skills.

Militarycareers.com (www.militarycareers.com). Interested recruits will find lots of branch-specific information that may help to determine which branch is the best fit.

Montgomery GI Bill (www.gibill.va.gov). Site explains this college tuition program available to all new recruits.

Naval Sea Cadet Corps (www.seacadets.org). Students between the ages of thirteen and seventeen can join up to learn about the navy SEALs and other naval organizations without military obligation.

Navy Recruitment Site (www.navy.com). Basic information for interested recruits.

Works Consulted

Books

Bruce Berkowitz, *The New Face of War: How War Will Be Fought in the 21st Century*. New York: Free Press, 2003. This book is intended to give readers a look at how the "information revolution" is changing war and what the United States must do to prepare for it.

David Bohrer, *America's Special Forces: Weapons, Missions, Training*. St. Paul, MN: MBI, 2002. This oversized book is full of 4-color photos of aircraft, weapons, and soldiers in various aspects of training.

Hugh McManners, *Ultimate Special Forces*. New York: DK Publishing, 2003. This book highlights the world's modern special forces and includes numerous photographs of equipment and weapons.

Periodicals

Don Stauffer, "Electronic Warfare: Battles Without Bloodshed," *Futurist*, January 2000.

Pat Wingert, Donatella Lorch, and Andrew Murr, "The War of the Night: Special Forces Open the Ground War. The Making of Elite Fighters—and the Battle They Face," *Newsweek*, October 29, 2001.

Internet Sources

Air Force News Service, "Air Force Snipers in Iraq," August 6, 2003. http://usmilitary.about.com/cs/airforce/a/afsniper2.htm.

Airman, "No Wimps Allowed," 2000. www.specialoperations. com/Schools/AFSOC/Airman_Magazine.htm.

David Best, "Consider Staying in the Active Army," VetJobs. com. http://63.243.14.115/military.htm.

Jake Boerhave, "Marine Recon," *Profile*, April 2003. www.spear. navy.mil/profile/April2003.pdf.

Danielle Burrows and Tim Barela, "Surviving Terrorism,"

Airman, September 2002. www.af.mil/news/airman/0902/con sumer.html.

GoArmy.com, "Special Forces Overview: Your Most Powerful Weapon Is Your Mind." http://banner.goarmy.com/banrtrck/ banrdocs/armyop49.jsp;jsessionid=5413CF69EB5C2E7DFB5 339E4A23AA6C7?banner=3662-016i-9999-9999-49.

Martin Jackson, "Fly Away Security Teams (FAST)," Air Force News Service. http://usmilitary.about.com/od/airforce/a/affast. htm.

Mark Kinkade, "The Future of Flight," Air Force News Service, January 2004. http://usmilitary.about.com/cs/weapons/a/future flight.htm.

Kelly Luster, "Army Military Police (MPs) Deployed," Army News Service, February 16, 2004. http://usmilitary.about. com/cs/army/a/ardeployedmp.htm.

Pat McKenna, "Quoth the Ravens, 'Nevermore,'" *Airman*, November 1997. www.af.mil/news/airman/1197/raven2.htm.

Navy News Service, "Basic Enlisted Submarine School (BESS)." http://usmilitary.about.com/od/navytrng/a/bess.htm?terms=m ilitary+navy+electronics+training+.

—————, "Retention Incentive Pays for Special Operations Forces," February 2005. http://usmilitary.about.com/od/mili tarypay/a/specoppay.htm.

Navy.com, "Careers: Aviation." www.navy.com/jsp/career/career _details.jsp?cid=2&pid=1.

Navy.com, "Careers: Electronics." www.navy.com/enlisted/elec tronics.

Rod Powers, "U.S. Military Special Operations Forces," About. com. http://usmilitary.about.com/od/jointservices/a/specialops. htm.

TodaysMilitary.com, "Discussion #3: Employers' Views on Veterans." www.todaysmilitary.com/discstarters/views_vets.pdf.

Jason Tudor, "Air Force Countersnipers: Eyeing the Sights," *Airman*. http://usmilitary.about.com/library/milinfo/milarticles/ blafsnipers.htm.

"U.S. Military Navy SEAL Training: Reinventing BUD/S." http://usmilitary.about.com/cs/navy/a/navyseal.htm.

"U.S. Military: SEAL Training Hell Week" http://usmilitary.about. com/od/navytrng/a/sealhellweek.htm.

Robert Valdes, "How Military Snipers Work," HowStuffWorks. com. http://science.howstuffworks.com/sniper.htm.

White House, "President Addresses the Nation." www.white house.gov/news/releases/2003/09/20030907-1.html.

Index

Picture Credits

Cover image: © CORBIS
Ali Hader/EPA/Landov, 31
AP/Wide World Photos, 68
© Bob Daemmrich/CORBIS, 12
© Brownie Harris/CORBIS, 20
© CORBIS, 83
© Corel Corporation, 54, 61, 67, 74, 79, 80, 89
Ed Kashi/CORBIS, 24
© George Hall/CORBIS, 47, 71
Getty Images, 9, 34, 49, 56, 72
Kim Ludbrook/EPA/Landov, 40
© Leif Skoogfors/CORBIS, 37, 86
© Lester Lefkowitz/CORBIS, 58
Lynsey Addario/CORBIS, 35
Najlah Feanny/SABA/CORBIS, 32
Sandy Huffacker/ZUMA/CORBIS, 85
T. Mughal/EPA/Landov, 15
UPI/Landov, 18, 19

About the Author

Sheri Bell-Rehwoldt is the author of two other titles in Lucent's Careers for the Twenty-First Century series: *Art* and *Law*. A member of the American Society of Journalists and Authors, she has penned numerous articles on the arts, health, human resources, and interesting people and places for Web sites and national, trade, and regional publications, including *American Profile*, *Family Circle*, *HR Innovator*, *Ladies' Home Journal*, *Mobil Travel Guide*, and *Ripley's Believe It or Not*. She also writes and edits for business and nonprofit clients.